A Year on Facebook:

a quixotic monologue

Personal reflections on cinema, the arts, life and

political philosophy

ADDIE ALKHAS

ISBN:1496006011
ISBN-13: 978-1496006011

DEDICATION

This book is dedicated to mama and papa.

The Internet has become the opium of the masses.

James Petras

ADDIE ALKHAS

By 1845 Marx and Engels had developed the materialist conception of history, which established that revolutions are not the product of well-organized conspiracies carried out by determined leaders and their followers. They are the necessary outcome of a complex socioeconomic process, in which the development of the productive forces comes into irrepressible conflict with the existing social relations within which they had heretofore developed. Thus, the source of revolution was to be found not in the movement of ideas, but in the socioeconomic organization of society, conditioned by a certain level of the development of the productive forces. The contradiction between the development of the productive forces and the existing social relationships finds political expression in the class struggle, which in modern society assumes the principal form of the conflict between the bourgeoisie, which owns the means of production, and the proletariat, the working class, which possesses only its ability to work.

David North

ACKNOWLEDGMENTS

Thanks to Shawn Deena and Kayte Thomas for their help in editing this small book..

PREFACE

"The weapon of criticism cannot, of course, replace criticism by weapons, material force must be overthrown by material force; but theory also becomes a material force as soon as it has gripped the masses ... as philosophy finds its material weapons in the proletariat, so the proletariat finds its spiritual weapons in philosophy." Karl Marx

Idealism may have a place but it should be made obedient to the rule of facts through a process of reflection and inquiry on these otherwise it is romanticism of the most ruinous of sorts. And in the investigation of social relations rather than using the term leftist which has taken on an unjustly derogatory perspective from

1

a popular sense it would be more correct to state its obvious social character more in line with the needs of and in reference to the working class and the class struggle in general. Such terms like the middle class, liberal and conservative, or the left and right intentionally lack sufficient clarity to give context to their social reference.

With these opening remarks I must begin by trying to explain how this book came to be as well as how these remarks reflect on the purpose of my book. I have always found that once I write down my thoughts, the words begin to take on a more profound urgency. Certainly, there is that urgency to give a permanent expression to ideas, attitudes and principles that in large part have shaped me. But now, these words exist outside of me and much like the counsel I offer my children, I can't be there to ensure their reception is met according to my intentions. I am filled with a paralyzing sense of audacity and the ridiculous arises in me when I consider such a venture. I understand this to be from a lack of any authority or a platform on which to bring this authority to my words. Who am I to challenge the system or raise the sound of alarm to a world thrown into chaos? And yet, quixotically, I am convinced of their importance and necessity or at least the processes that brought me to embrace this need for inquiry, reflection and analysis. So then, where are the windmills?

More precisely the genesis of this book is tied to the completion of my father's book (*Faking Honesty* by Marduk Alkhas) sometime in June of 2012 essentially working on editorial changes and formatting thereafter. By that time I was deeply engaged in my own personal readings on various topics such as art history and politics as a byproduct of the research I had been doing to complete the unfinished manuscript. The emotional residue that remained in the months following eventually turned into Facebook musings simply to vent my thoughts and feelings. Naïvely, it seemed to provide a purpose beyond casual usage: I thought provocation would spur challenges and discussions and slowly create a circle of interest. Here was a medium through which ideas, dialogues and community could be readily fostered. I was in need for such dialogue but lacking any understanding of social media nor appreciating its far too often superficial usage I soon realized I was carrying on more of a discouraging monologue. I should know better that in a world filled with distractions the internet will, as Petras asserted, offer little to people looking for more distraction. But in the end even Don Quixote recovered from his stupor before he died.

In many ways this foolishness I call my idealism is like a rusty suit of armor my father gave me. I wear it proudly as a way of remembering the life he forged for his family. But these ideals, the optimism that believes people have the capacity to eventually understand their social conditions and collectively begin the movement away from perilous reactions to a thoughtful organization of their resources in a sustainable and equitable fashion, also carry conditions. It is for having the courage to stand by them and allowing them to guide you. My Facebook monologues were in some sense the continuation of what I had finished and what I had wished not to finish.

As the months were passing and I had my father's book finally published, the thought of converting my Facebook posts into a short book came to me. And what I found interesting about

Facebook and social media writing is that the form is essentially designed and suitable for creating poetic-prose texts; vignettes, aphorisms and brief essays. There is no real room for long drawn out or well-articulated position statements as the content only holds the reader's attention for the briefest moment. It reminded me of a digital version of my own habit of writing ideas or thoughts in the margins of my books that a passage in my reading led me to. (At times I have borrowed excerpts directly from my readings. The sources have been cited accordingly. These often times did not make it into Facebook posts due to their length.) Most of my posts came from these as well as reflections on current events depicted in the news. Although Facebook is a public forum, the public has seemingly little patience or desire to participate beyond casual interactions. This is not to be critical of the public but, like the characters of Cervantes book, they live in the far too real imposition of the form on the content. *"Too much sanity may be madness and maddest of all, to see life as it is and not as it should be."* (*Don Quixote* by Miguel de Cervantes Saavedra) Even when I read Cervantes' book, which is now 400 years old, it still has the poignancy of what I would call a modern novel. Its episodic narrative offers more commentary on the social aspects while the characters of Don Quixote and Sancho Panza act as facilitators. Arguably, Cervantes' decrepit hero possesses a quality much more important than practicality (touch with reality) that makes him appear more human and sympathetic than mad or comical. He challenges the insanity of such a practicality. But a monologue remains a mad man's utterings unless someone will listen.

The main purpose of this book has been a personal assimilation of history, politics and arts and their present evolution into our development or broader understanding of events. To the extent that Marx remains, despite more than a century of our capitalist milieu, despite an onslaught of vehement opposition and misunderstood ravings, foremost, at the forefront of political and economic thought it has been as a student of Marx in contextualizing for me the ideas behind structures and the imposition of form on content. This riddle of dialectic materialism has been the main focus of these musings. In part it is as I had noted in my father's book the story of power relations and the quote by Marx at the beginning is its succinct political expression.

However it remains for each of us to decipher these for ourselves. And without embarking on this necessary reflection, we are often lulled into making and repeating our errors.

JUNE

Prologue: There is no such a thing as a beginning …

There are perhaps kernels of social truth in both religion and materialism from a consumerist perspective but their ultimate expressions are false and a point of oscillation between one to the other from a historical perspective. One offers moral rigidity and a sense of permanence but causes creative stagnation while the other teeters on over indulgence of the senses without appreciation for the cause and effect. Religion and consumerism are the two faces of the same coin. They exalt humanity falsely even if they vehemently deny it. They are both from a broad perspective selfish in their approach because they lack critical inquiry for the intolerance they preach. Morality is not necessarily a religious domain nor does it have some supremacy over it, and the current approach to materialism is not abstracted into an intellectual conception of what it means to meet basic but balanced human needs. One seeks the hereafter and the other immediate gratification. They are both in essence static. However, the inability to concede the limitations in both facets creates an inability to seek an alternate course. It is the ultimate intellectual crisis that has faced mankind. We need to abstract towards realism and not mystification.

The bonds between carbon, oxygen, hydrogen and nitrogen are in themselves moral, do possess life, and can be the basis for a narrative.

Arnold Hauser, art historian, makes an important distinction about the duality of religion and political realism from the basis of their power structures. In both situations you have the propaganda of elite classes separating the social-individual into a physical and meta-physical entity. Neither is based on abstraction towards realism; rather towards mystification. The religious zealots place focus towards the subjugation of the will-soul, while materialists are consumed by the power of material conquest through subjugation of surplus value-labor. Marxist theory and principles regarding the social-individual speaks to the domination of materialism over mankind in a historical context. Religion then is a component of this materialist description. Key to the idea of the social-individual is the word social and our inter-relationship with our biosphere. Our diverse disciplines have taken a detached approach to the truths of our lives. The patterns we discover, the relationships we decipher carry with them a much deeper rationale...we are intimately connected to the biosphere and do not possess a moral superiority. Delusions about material or religious imperatives may make us feel safe but they remain delusions and seed of our downfall. If our conscience can appreciate the interrelationship of the biosphere then 'it' should impose a moral constraint upon us. Our realities should teach us how to be.

When abstracting [communication forms] favor giving clarity to realism. Be very careful to not mystify reality.

When the end justifies the means, the methods used to achieve them gain independent justification. Methodology is important to a correct assessment of the ends. (See *dialectic materialism*)

It isn't just their problem ... it is our problem just as much as our successes are a by-product of the support of many others ... *"an injury to one is an injury to all."*

We are struggling with the fatigue of chronic violence that imposes itself through every crisis we have experienced.

Representative Democracy is a cautionary tale. There is no substitute for a dynamic participatory democracy and process. Unions, despite polar arguments for or against them, offer working people a structure through which they can participate. Even the possibility of reforming them from their current degeneration is better than having none in existence. The history of advances of unions in the U.S. work place is something few people know about. In this context the Wisconsin election and the methods that could ensure Mitt Romney's assumption of the presidency will have dire social consequences as is evident by current continuing economic events in Asia, Europe and U.S. The creation of jobs, the building of our infrastructures, investment in our children's education, creation of sound medical institutions directly linked through research labs, pharmaceuticals and medical schools, etc., is vitally necessary and must be divorced of Wall Street profit motives. There is no need to connect Wall Street's money to job creation processes, but this can only be achieved through a dynamic participatory process that is open and transparent.

Every neuron in our body is drug dependent.

All love stories are about how two wrongs made a right.

Be careful of absolutist tendencies. The frame of reference in our historical motion swore the sun rose and set.

We are pattern recognition learners. It must be a part of our circadian rhythm.

I heard someone is starting a new campaign to raise funds for endangered species. It seems in these trying economic times the number of rich people is declining drastically. Romney is their poster child.

NPR said that the middle class lost 35% of their net worth in the recession. But the top 10% gained. This should be construed as a "transfer" of wealth.

The dominance of aesthetics in art is suggestive of its external value as an art object commoditized. The aesthetics should be subservient to the purpose of the text in its communicative intent. Then we can begin to appreciate its internal value. Beauty is, in other words, a ruse.

Without historical context and relevance our words drift in a sea of alphabet soup sticking to nothing but the side of the soon to be empty bowl. Become your own journalist; dig into issues and find their deep rooted connections. Be cautious of nationalistic fervor and adulterated patriotism. Our allegiances often come with a personal price. It is easy to lose ourselves in the static of

A YEAR ON FACEBOOK

disheartening noise. But there is an abundance of silence in the historical context.

Every aggressor postures as a defender; it is true of school yard bullies and true of warring nations.

Don't pick and choose the facts. If your narrative explanations of the facts don't conform to all the facts verified then the explanation is wrong. This is where we constantly fail. This is true in science. It is applicable to our life.

There have been 40,000 generations of humans on this planet. They are the sum of all that we are and yet we know so little about them.

It is easier to take apart than to build. It is easier to sow discontent than foster camaraderie. It is easier to forget than to remember. But we have a great capacity to get up again, wipe the dirt off and begin rebuilding.

The narrative thread in the 60-second political campaign ad is capriciously devoid of substance but aesthetically charged for emotion. It is the exemplary format demonstrating how the cinematic form creates content while relying on realism to compel our intellect in believing the fiction. Always, always, remember that all art texts are subjective.

A fact (one) is a truth. Two facts become the subjective interpretation of the truth.

Don't outsource your conscience ... It's a disservice to you and others.

Truth in content can't be distinguished from truth in form. This can perhaps best be appreciated by understanding *individualism* within its social context. However, there is a tendency to separate the individual from a social conception and we begin to lose sight of what is important and necessary. The study or art and history have always fought (for or against) distinguishing these. And yet it is precisely in attempting to comprehend this fusion of the individual in society that our understanding of current politics and economics can begin to assume a more realistic, urgent and possibly constructive direction. Thus far we have relegated ourselves to a constant evaluation of emotional fodder while lacking the ability to understand the impact of past and present structures on our current social content. In short, we remain reactive in our conclusions, our approaches and solutions. Our general acceptance and desensitization to violence and violent solutions at all levels speaks to this.

Tomorrow never really arrives. It stands beyond arm's length always taunting. Today stays by your side through the good and bad. I like today.

Unemployment is holding steady...Under-employment is continuing to rise.

After receiving an extracellular growth signal, the retinoblastoma molecule disassociates from E2F after being phosphorylated by Cyclin D-CDK4 allowing the HDA reductase enzyme to release the histones from the chromatin and initiate the Cell cycle through G1 phase to enter S phase and replicate the DNA. The republicans then pass a bill to cut all funding to all social programs promoting P53 arrest of the cell cycle before it advances thru the S-phase.

It's easy for elephants to ignore the elephant in the room.

One of the biggest social misconceptions perpetuated has been the pairing of poverty and laziness. It is so rampant and pervasive that it has become accepted as a truism without appreciating its falsity and maliciousness. It is from this perspective that we should consider the current economic and political turmoil.

The truth doesn't hurt. The illusion it peels off is the source of the pain.

Artists? We relished their aesthetics but negated their rhetoric, erased their names and romanticized their history.

Myths that come closer to reality are far more vexing and insidious. Their perpetuation is a mode of indoctrination and a framework for propaganda. Criticism of them meets with seething vitriol. Illusions seem to have a compelling psychological salve. It affords a semblance of control over chaos. Though even the ancients thought the gods held up the sky these new myths are as close to reality as those ancient divinely supported skies.

JULY

Humans possess an abundance of drama in their life but life is never a dramatic process. This creates much of our seeming contradictions.

We have a very hard time figuring out our "selves."

Trotsky: Appealing to "inconsistency" as justification for an unprincipled theoretical bloc signifies giving oneself bad credentials as a Marxist. Inconsistency is not accidental, and in politics it does not appear solely as an individual symptom.

Inconsistency usually serves a social function. There are social groupings which cannot be consistent. Petty-bourgeois elements who have not rid themselves of hoary petty-bourgeois tendencies are systematically compelled within a workers' party to make theoretical compromises with their own conscience ... Our scientific thinking is only a part of our general practice including techniques. For concepts there also exits 'tolerance' which is established not by formal logic issuing from the axiom 'A' is equal to 'A', but by the dialectical logic issuing from the axiom that everything is always changing. 'Common sense' is characterized by the fact that it systematically exceeds dialectical 'tolerance'. Vulgar thought operates with such concepts as capitalism, morals, freedom, workers' state, etc. as fixed abstractions, presuming that capitalism is equal to capitalism. Morals are equal to morals, etc. Dialectical thinking analyzes all things and phenomena in their continuous change, while determining in the material conditions of those changes that critical limit beyond which 'A' ceases to be 'A', a workers' state ceases to be a workers' state ... Dialectical thinking is related to vulgar in the same way that a motion picture is related to a still photograph. The motion picture does not outlaw the still photograph but combines a series of them according to the laws of motion. Dialectics does not deny the syllogism, but teaches us to combine syllogisms in such a way as to bring our understanding closer to the eternally changing reality. Hegel in his logic established a series of laws: change of quantity into quality, development through contradictions, conflict of content and form, interruption of continuity, change of possibility into inevitability, etc., which are just as important for theoretical thought as is the simple syllogism for more elementary tasks... We call it our dialectic materialist, since its roots are neither in heaven nor in the depths of our "free will", but in objective reality, in nature. Consciousness grew out of the unconscious, psychology out of physiology, the organic world out of the inorganic, and the solar system out of the nebulae.

On all the rungs of this ladder of development, the quantitative changes were transformed into qualitative. Our thought, including dialectical thought, is only one of the forms of the expression of changing matter. There is place within this system for neither god nor devil, nor immortal soul, nor eternal norms of laws and morals. The dialectic of thinking, having grown out of the dialectic of nature, possesses consequently a thoroughly materialist character... Marx, who in distinction from Darwin was a conscious dialectician, discovered a basis for the scientific classification of human societies in the development of their productive forces and the structure of the relations of ownership which constitute the anatomy of society. Marxism substituted for the vulgar descriptive classification of societies and states, which even up to now still flourishes in the universities, a materialistic dialectical classification. Only through using the method of Marx is it possible correctly to determine both the concept of a workers' state and the moment of its downfall. *Trotsky 1939 (In defense of Marx)*

The current nature of Trotsky's explanation of dialectic thought and dialectic materialism is central to all our current political issues. Without the ability to understand the current processes taking place then where are we? It is important to be able to give a precise description to this. One has to see the centrality of revolution to society and the discipline amongst the rank as the living embodiment of this permanent revolution he emphasized; permanent because it is not a process that occurs outside of us but rather a relationship of people with each other. It is the vigilance of maintaining these relationships. Discipline does not necessarily imply subordination. On the contrary it implies active participation. In as much as the scientific method allows giving form to phenomenon, it also allows us to communicate this form and replicate and test it to further analyze and decipher it. The dialectic method is this process applied to social movements. Materialistic dialectics is not simply a description of economics; it is a basis for the development of our social character. We are the byproduct of our social movements.

Every genuine artist moves towards the truth through a relative sense. It is always the motion of things that has to be appreciated. All (art) forms possess the ability to capture the motion of their content. They describe them, articulate them, or even crystallize them (in photographic motion.) This is true for all disciplines; perhaps most in understanding historical truths. Nothing is static.

The Scientific Method and Dialectic Method; the first observes the concrete and the other the abstract but both are grounded in realism in so much as they clarify and give form to phenomenon. The ability to study the form of this phenomenon is what allows us to make correct conclusions and posit appropriate questions. It is also important to note that drama and emotional fodder arises through them as well -- they are not devoid of the experience -- they are not cold and without feeling. However, as we are buried in mysticism, they are alien to our conception of pragmatic but emotive narrative constructions and, so, we shun their potentials. Nonetheless, these remain the two most important methodologies we have developed to give a correct conscious perspective to this so called life and its motions. The sooner we adopt them, embrace their constant correction to our errors, then the sooner we will distance ourselves from our present destructive and excessive pathways.

All people who seek power have a fear complex.

We have to maintain a healthy cautious attitude when studying history through all the formal tools in our possession - books, paintings, film, etc. The study of history is flat; it lacks temporal significance for us because of the condensation of the historical process into subjective abstraction based on various facts. There is a discontinuity of the experiences because of the assimilation of time into its distant singularity we know as history. The process happens for us all at once through a secondary medium beyond our experience of it. Though the analysis may be correct the conclusions and lessons can lose their past evolving characteristics and its impressions fall "flat" upon us. Therefore (in the study of history) its relevance can only become apparent in its ability to give detached clarity to our present. The dialectic method in its relativistic approach to historic motion gives the needed breadth for this clarity and including the development of necessary and correct hypotheses that attempts to understand the "now." It is necessary to understand the motion of concepts not their static imprint. With a nod to cinema, its power is recognizably most profound in its form centered dialectic capacity.

The development of a communicative-approach and purpose to perspective in art created the ability for a "formal" reach to the infinite. The stylistic symbolism of placing images proximal to each other gave way to the development of "continuity in content" through perspective. It emphasized the negative space within and beyond the frame of reference. This evolution was most profound during the baroque period when Copernicus rediscovered that the sun and not the earth was the center of the solar system. The scientific discovery created a revolution in "thought" that shattered religious dogma of man's proximity with god. It forced a reconfiguration of the interpretation of the infinite but silent cosmos and man's place within it. The formal use of exaggerated perspective in the artistic styles of the period became an expression of this philosophical shift in thought. Today we find ourselves insulated from such shifts in thought despite our scientific discoveries. We are thoroughly immunized. There is a deep acceptance despite our resistance or irritations with the present processes. The haves care little of eroding infrastructures that give so much important content to our lives. Many believe it is a political process. Many believe, despite repeated historical precedence, that private enterprise will FIX it all. Many rewind time when the US invested in the welfare state and see the past as good and the present as bad. There has been, in the last 20 years, a deep rooted belief that poverty is synonymous to laziness, ugliness, unworthiness. We are suspicious of each other. Current popular politics polarizes and polarizes ad infinitum. There is no cohesion. There is no perspective. And soon they will be selling the fragmented wind.

A welfare state is a "concept of government in which the state plays a key role in the protection and promotion of the economic and social well-being of its citizens. It is based on the principles of equality of opportunity, equitable distribution of wealth, and public responsibility for those unable to avail themselves of the minimal provisions for a good life. The general term may cover a variety of forms of economic and social organization." But it is a far cry from a worker's state.

Currently, in the U.S., welfare is not considered a part of education and healthcare with regards to GDP spending assessment. It entails $450 billion which for the most part are part of the tax rebates we get, unemployment checks and assistance and temporary assistance to needy families. Education is a mere $150 billion with a significant portion to vocational schools and higher education financial assistance. Healthcare comes second at $850 billion behind defense which is at its highest ever at $900 billion. Sixty percent of healthcare goes to seniors and about 30% goes to states as grants for Medicaid. Social expenditure as part of GDP: US ranks #26 at 14.8% behind many European countries we supposedly admire. Ranked at the top are Sweden and Denmark are near 30%. There GDP per capita is essentially equivalent to ours. We currently pay $224 billion in interest. In summary, defense spending continues to increase now at $900 billion. Gross

public debt is at $16 trillion. Call it a pickle.

TUG

One of eight million species that call earth home

We are seven billion plus populating this blue sphere the third

from the sun

Spinning with our sister planets in a seemingly eternal waltz

Poised at the edge of the milky way galaxy in our quiet solar

system

One amongst a billion others - a sorority of galactic cousins

Joined in the gravitational tug of a billion other galaxies

That swim bright in the so called heavens

One night sky just the utterance of a faint syllable in the cosmic

lullaby

It is not who controls capital but who capital controls. This

relationship is much more complex and in line with realties. This requires seeing capital as a social entity that has a life of its own and reflects structural motion predicting content.

The more I understand the more I realize the direction of things is the opposite of our logic - where our logic is from inside out, our realities are from the outside in. We are always reactionary. People who handle capital are reactionary. Naturally, we are persuaded by the growth of capital and therefore we ignore, down play, and turn a blind eye from the havoc it causes to our social inter-relationships including the ecosystem in its broadest sense. Capital imposes its rule on us in a very deep and troubling sense.

The parliamentary development in the late 17th century in England and for that matter the revolutions in France and Americas in the second half of the 18th century were predominately of bourgeois character. The economic developments led to the centralization of real power in a few people with control of the economically productive elements of society. The parliament, as a social structure, guaranteed the transfer of executive and judicial powers from the nobility/royalty to the bourgeois elements. What it also provided was the development of a pseudo-democratic structure necessitated from gaining the assurance of the working classes as partners in a new social contract and of course, with it, the elements in artistic development that relate to realism. Making money has to be a practical matter. However, the premise of this contract did not operate on freedoms but right to freedoms based on economic merit which translated to securing economic possessions. The parliament also ensured no one person within the privileged class would assert or usurp power from their brethren. What seems to have assured England's royal house survival is acceptance of the parliament's rule which at the same time garnered parliament historical legitimacy in the eyes of the nation and world. Our present historical evolution of democracy has been based on the economic basis of capital's rule and dominance. However, as we have socially evolved in these last three centuries, there has remained a growing antagonism between capital and people that has resulted in so many of the revolutions since as well as movements that have attempted to expose Capital's coercive influence while attempting to obtain real and practical freedoms for the people - equal rights for women, denouncement of racial bigotry, acceptance of gender issues as well as liberating social institutions such as medicine and education that have heightened and given life a palpable zest and comfort. However, as corporate evolution has become international and autocratic, the democracy that has been established is becoming the ultimate propagandist tool to muddy the real issues. Naturally, the political diatribes between the liberals and conservative, as much of a circus show they were with the Whigs and Tories, remains a ruse, a distraction from the real issues. Certainly, corporate monarchism has evolved into an explicit coercive tendency while the rhetoric of democratic rules attempt to dispel revolutionary development. The question that arises is if our personal survival becomes dependent on accepting class distinctions and privileges, what will people choose - a re-evaluation of true democratic rights and freedoms or the crumbs from the corporate windows upon the favored?

Conquer and divide by dispensing privilege. Dispense privilege and people will divide on their own volition.

JOY

With eager exuberance my joy seeks a voice,

But a formidable cocoon of apathy has contained it

Permeating from me only a false sense of anguish and ire

Deep into the world

AUGUST

There is a crisis of social identity that is inflicting western civilizations of Europe and America and the world at large. It is an inability to place ourselves in the context of our present thus unable to form rational solutions to the immediate needs of the future. This stems from our rhetorical nature. We idealize; we are poetic and emotional. However, rather than realizing the realities that face us, we grasp at the romanticized notions of the past not recognizing that it has actually been the real and developed ideas of the past that have gotten us here. Paul Ryan's televised speech (He was picked as Romney's choice for VP) may have been construed as powerful by the "right wing" media. Arguably it was evocative. But his euphemisms were lies lingering in the shades of truths. "But America is more than just a place ... it's an idea. It's the only country founded on an idea. Our rights come from nature and God, not government. We promise equal opportunity, not equal outcomes." Contextually these words sound appealing but remain fallacious. Factually, the ideas behind these words are attributable to John Locke in his *Second Treatise of Civil Government*. To understand Locke's ideas, his rationale, the development of his ideas of our present democracy and its emphasis on the individual requires a broad evaluation of the evolution of mercantilism into industrial market economies. We are far from John Smith's belief that selfishness and personal interests were sufficient real motives for the development of a free market economy. Such free markets, such individualism, no longer exist despite the decrying by FOX news and the socially conservative base such as the Tea Party. Current market realities obviously are the basis for much of the troubles that have interjected themselves over the last one hundred years. However, at the phase of each social movement, the markets have commandeered the social instruments and given it a rhetorical bent absorbing the thrusts that have opposed it. Our social identity crisis arises from our romanticizing the individual into its absolute ideal. So my question is, what can this promise of equal opportunity be other than the rhetoric of more of the same?

The potential for sentimentalism and emotionalism in the fictional drama can blur realities. It is a dangerous matter that belief in the emotions becomes synonymous with the truth of the issues. The facts should elicit the emotions rather than emotionalizing the facts. Otherwise our fear of the night would imply a monster lurks under our bed.

Social Static-ism is the inability to see the imperceptible motion in social and political processes which leads to erroneous and false conclusions and therefore an inability of the social organism to see or understand itself. Historically, laws attributable to God and Nature have suffered from this.

A VERY SHORT STORY: A man was falling to his death when his mind suddenly turned to his friends and the family he knew. He thought it was odd that at this moment all these memories were rushing to the forefront of his conscious each vying for his attention when before he had given them little thought. He was quite perplexed, distraught and anxious overcome with tender emotions. But then the ground appeared very quickly. THE END

We use volume to utter our position. Volume has become our position.

Intellectualism in defense of elitism is empty rhetoric of the shallowest magnitude.

Unsettlingly, our social collective efforts focus on using the same tools to "fix" the problems that have landed us here.

Alternative solutions are necessary but these are considered heresy even at the subconscious level. We who need these solutions most are often the first to oppose them. But this opposition is not borne in us. It is a byproduct of a social collective educational process that suppresses creative energies that run counter to the "fix." Fundamentally, we are extremely homogenized because we have accepted the conveniences of the process we are bound to.

What we see most often precedes what we understand. For the artist in revolution these occur simultaneously. This is what they mean when they say she is ahead of her time.

When I watch a film I first watch it as an idiot. My emotions will intuitively respond. Then I begin to analyze these stirrings and what led to them. Then the film begins to open itself to me.

There are so many distractions from the real.

Violence has become disturbingly soothing.

A mistake can become the most real thing in an art text.

Consider something simple as a uniform made from something no more than light cloth. More than making other people know who you are affiliated with it has tremendous weight in shaping your own values and attitudes. It subtly defines the impact of structure on your content. How are we to think of police hosing down protesting pedestrians or soldiers marching in the streets of foreign countries?

" ... I kill what I eat and what I eat kills me ..." (from the documentary film *Hecho in Mexico*)

FORM is heritable. CONTENT is not. FORM develops CONTENT and has tremendous influence on how it is perceived. The cyclic nature of history when viewed through the window of a milieu is a byproduct of FORM-mechanisms in place that give motion to societal events. There is the appearance of repetition. It is for this reason that the study of the French Revolution and the historical events following provide insight into the radical departure from medieval history. The contradictions in the previous milieu led to catastrophic structural changes from without and within creating the beginning of a new milieu. The unusual logic then is that though content is derived from broader FORMal structures in reality there is no such thing as content (as we have understood it.) CONTENT is FORM's reflection given intellectual awareness and preserved in textual constructs. FORM begets FORM and form will react against form.

The proletariat is the only human structure that exists. All other structures are external to human existence. It isn't composed of a group of leaders or a mass of people. The proletariat becomes a proletariat based on the social composition and purposeful action it applies itself to and this is to subjugate all external structures to its purpose and not counter to this against itself.

Though their work is fleeting the methods of a journalist are not dissimilar to those of an artist. However, given the nature of their work, the journalist is arguably more important from a temporal sense.

Spontaneity is a conventional response to convention.

Convention is dictated by the creation of necessity for said function (such as art) by a historic critical mass (people).

SEPTEMBER

We are the entertained. As we have been removed by the current politico-economic forces over the last few centuries from our labor, remaining foreign to it, separated from its communicative process, receiving the check as a form of gratitude, we have assumed the only status left to us – we the entertained. We seek it in every activity of our lives. Within our political process, our educational process, our workforce, etc. we have hollowed ourselves for its immediate gratification; lost the ability to analyze; lost the necessary critical thinking that can connect all present processes across geographic boundary and history. It has become an obligatory right to enjoy the pursuit of being entertained. This is equated with happiness. Yet, it is our labor, understanding its connection with life and its worth, its conscious influence that can bring us happiness. As consideration, a family unit is in itself nothing more than a procreative effort. The happiness and the real sense of a family begin in the realm of communication through dialogue, caress, supportive actions, etc. It is the labor of the family engaged in tending to its needs. It is this we have given up. We have accepted our reliance from above - from the government, from the entertainment industry or maybe from the hereafter heaven. No. Our entertainment is not happiness. It is a distraction. We seek distraction from the necessary things in life. We are unable to engage; we loath it. But it is precisely this that needs our attention; this apathy that needs to be cast out of us.

The powerlessness of the working classes stems from a social inferiority complex as manifested by a severely regressed political apathy. Political discourse was very rich and unifying more than a century ago with strong unions and small working class presses disseminating news and information. Today, this inferiority complex finds its relief through escapist behaviors and myth building. Media stories build only myths anymore. We don't even really have a national identity because we have sold it. We are recreating it digitally to appease the emptiness that consumption has consumed. Criticism is difficult to accept. It is abhorred. It is rejected because the reality of the predicament is emotionally disturbing. It only invites condemnation. But, by comparison, the Egyptian youths challenged and dared the military and their country's leaders with a moral authority and purpose not seen in a long time. It emboldened the disbelievers in their cause. They had little material wealth and political clout but nonetheless, when unified, demonstrated their inherent power. How that plays today and tomorrow we wait to see but their character showed itself. But this inferiority complex is destructive. What we possess is nothing if our character is void. We have to be collectively self-reliant. Not strength in pride but in solidarity. After all we are all people. We all share life in common.

All artistic movements have reflected both the changing social landscapes and the evolving relationship in the current milieu with consumers of her texts. We are transitioning to art as a craft again than as an expressive communicative process. Those choosing to believe in the language of their medium as an expression of their person must engage in annealing their conscious against a subconscious passiveness. It is more important than ever for the artist to remain resolute and innovative. She must explore this apathy.

DIGITAL vs. CELLULOID: The fake is the same.

Since the renaissance it has been the battle to shift from the concept of knowledge entrenched in its absolutist ideals to relativistic truths. Once absolutist tendencies take hold they are very difficult to shake off because we become attached to "absolute" narratives. This is organic to our species. This battle will, however, be the historical mark and defining transition for this millennium.

For the evaluation of inner-party blocs two questions are of decisive significance: (1) First and foremost against whom or what is the bloc directed? (2) What is the relationship of forces within the bloc? Thus for a struggle against chauvinism within one's own party a bloc between internationalists and centrists is wholly permissible. *The result of the bloc would in this case depend upon the clarity of the program of the internationalists, upon their* <u>*cohesiveness and discipline, for these traits are not infrequently more important in determining the relationship of forces than their numerical strength.*</u> - Leon Trotsky January 1940 - *In Defense of Marxism*

Sometimes we scream to hear our own voice. Sometimes we whisper it on the tail of a breeze to send it afar.

We focus on the action in our lives but we spend most of our time in between the scenes; from one room to another, in the hallways, in traffic, at the lights. But that is also where true feelings exist.

In a democracy - concerning the tripartite of liberty (freedom), fraternity, and equality - Fraternity has to stand above the other two. The other two can only arise from it. This misunderstanding lies at the contradiction of all democracies at present. We have unconsciously or consciously placed our personal freedoms above fraternity.

Don't just accept art texts (music, paintings, photographs, films, books, sculpting, etc.) as isolated pieces. They don't come with their social connections readily identifiable. Nonetheless their movements are a byproduct of social changes and the artist's relationship to these social stresses that affect her works.

Otherwise it will remain art for art's sake in a different sense than historically understood.

For many - obviously - food is a necessity. For a few it is a luxury.

The painter stands outside of the world of the canvas. The politician lives in it. He is part and parcel of the content.

A million opinions do not the truth make. Admitting our erroneous thoughts becomes vital in this sense.

Reality will guide your actions and be a better instinct than all your ideals and mistaken notions about said issues.

The great writers don't use powerful words. They use mundane ones placed in a specific order which impregnates them with forceful precision. In a manner this is what we mean by the difference between content and form. This is also socially and politically applicable.

Don't hold - clutch the paint brush.

On first look, asking someone to detach and engage in an art text is simply contradictory. Emphasizing emotional detachment and intellectual engagement however explicate this contradiction. If analysis and logic is at the forefront of this engagement, emotionalism can only blind or impair rationalism. Yet, the conclusion of the process requires to re-attach and disengage as the shared experience is now assimilated and the communicative purpose discovered and absorbed. This transformation makes it now personal. And this studied approach is necessary to repeat constantly as a means of aiding us when delving into social and political issues. We are part of this content and naturally react initially with an emotional expression. Identifying the source of these emotions is part of understanding who "we" are and not who "I" am. On a social canvas the "I"s are all connected into a complete text.

Snapshots: Capitalism in a country of clerical rule and religious dominance becomes a seeming beacon of cultural reform and progressiveness. Capital in a country whose saturated with labor and material wealth, whose cannibalizing itself to remain relevant becomes a cruel hoax and barbaric. These are phases; snapshots of capital's idealistic childhood and debilitated senile adulthood. This was what transpired in capital's initial development in western history without external structures to counter pose its systematic development. Capitalism for these new comers will be impeded and their growth stunted until their executors succumb.

It is important to understand why capital needs parliamentary democracy. This has to be worked out by each person engaging in any discussion on politics, economics and issues of social justice.

Inorganic structures take on a vital life force (become animated) through the activities of organic constituents. The imposition of quality by the inorganic on the organic life perpetuates their activities towards sustaining that inorganic life. The inorganic dictates.

The most mundane nondescript day to day meanderings of your life have the greatest influence on your deepest convictions.

OCTOBER

Gazing at the stars he fell into the black hole.

Individualism, nationalism, isolationism are siblings of the same misguided parent.

Blind nationalism is the seed of fascism; Economic crisis its spring well.

An artist that needs to speak defies convention. Those many that look for fame and financial rewards embrace it.

"In order that the social crisis may bring about the proletarian revolution, it is necessary that, besides other conditions, a decisive shift of the petty bourgeois classes occurs in the direction of the proletariat. This gives the proletariat a chance to put itself at the head of the nation as its leader. The last election (Germany 1931) revealed - and this is where its principal symptomatic significance lays - a shift in the opposite direction. Under the blow of the crisis, the petty bourgeoisie swung, not in the direction of the proletarian revolution, but in the direction of the most extreme imperialist reaction, pulling behind it considerable sections of the proletariat." Trotsky

In countries where the petite-bourgeoisie is a functioning and established class/social entity then its alignment will be with the bourgeoisie elements because its experience stems from it. They aren't natural allies – they can have a quite antagonistic relationship – but their alignment makes them a function of bourgeoisie control. They must abandon their capitalistic historical preconditions and forge a force under the leadership of the proletariat bringing its skills and development in the service of developing the socialist preconditions. If it attempts to usurp this leadership of the proletariat on the morning after the revolution then it will remain as a reactionary force that eradicates proletarian action to re-establish Capital's dominance. At present, the petite-bourgeoisie is essentially the middle class, the term most familiar currently. They have also been established as the engine of capital's consumerist endeavor which has broader implications; apathy for political process, subordination to economic directions, and complicity in environmental devastation, to name a few.

One function of the state is to protect the bourgeoisie when the petite bourgeoisie is non-existent which has appeared in underdeveloped nations under a capitalist milieu as well as in totalitarian/bureaucratic states where the proletariat's position has been idealized but its actual function marginalized. Its other function in countries where the economy and capital have developed to a great extent is to subdue and direct the petite-bourgeoisie as a buffer to and indicator of capital's creation of social crisis. In proletariat revolutions it is to give a structural apparatus for their expression as a new entity in control of the productive forces of the nation. In a world ruled under the domain of capital the morning after the revolution becomes the next most important event as the crisis of counter-revolution is eminent externally and internally. The leadership of this movement has the monumental task of pursuing the permanent revolution beyond its borders and within its self. It has to develop into an organic expression of it otherwise the betrayal lurks in the subconscious.

We all eat. However, how (including what) we eat is in large part a reflection of our social relationships.

We (need to) confront/deal with issues that are most urgently (in the) present.

What is our fascination with social media other than a confrontation with the extreme isolation that our individualism has forced us into.

"...there still remains, as the only task worth attempting, the need to distinguish precisely the historical roles of the individual and the super-individual, and to do justice to them both without slipping into a mystical conception of either or, as so generally happens, of both." Arnold Hauser

We have to own responsibility.

In a capitalist milieu equality stands as a seemingly absolute contradiction. Privilege has become its proxy and the pursuit of privilege its meaning.

There are no individual aims. There are only social aims that take on individual variations.

Efficiency is a process of simplification through dissection while understanding is the process of integration into the complex. This combination of process is how abstraction is born.

Efficiency, from its practical aspects, can have tremendous immediate results while oftentimes at great "social" costs. Though we seem to lack this capacity, it is important to give primary importance to such cost assessments. Vertically integrated infra-structures provide such efficiency while horizontal-human connections are purposefully fractured. As such, true accounts of these are given expression through crises.

Permanent revolution is the answer to permanent crisis.

Striving for efficiency in social movements will create impediments to its progress. This has been the source of violence and rhyme.

Structure communicates vertically while content horizontally. All vertical communications are therefore coded because our senses can only discern content – a horizontal framework. Our brains have the capacity to reintegrate the data and give an ideation of the vertical experience.

An artistic solution to a problem is the process of finding a way to transform an idea into a communicated expression.

However, the codes contained in the expression (art text) will still need to be worked out by the receiver of the expression.

All art texts project what is internal to the artist unto a form (medium) for reception. The film uses a projector and screen. The music uses musicians and turns notes into sound. The writer uses words unto a page. In theater the actor's pretense supplements a straight read. His pretense is no more than projection. In film he is less ... a projected albeit protected image.

Even the methods used to achieve results are conditioned by results that direct the methods.

It is rare for content to be spontaneous and unconventional. Experiences are common and shared across space and time. Therefore spontaneity in form becomes the momentary substitute and surrogate for emphasizing and reinvigorating through its ability to deceive. But here in lies the riddle of Sisyphus his self-deception. Every art form has been a form of deception by idealizing reality through the perpetual interplay of originality and convention. We have always struggled against seeing the inevitable futility; the struggle becoming the purpose. But it remains my belief that within the struggle the rock will eventually come to rest on that crest. The re-experience of experience will create new content in the context of that struggle.

Environmentalism is a luxury of rich countries.

Sociologically and psychologically there is a difference between conceiving the artist as a worker than as an idol.

NOVEMBER

Habit is experience without the realization of its impact or magnitude because of its repetitive nature. It becomes the negative space on our personal canvas. Social structures have their own habits. But they can be counterproductive to action or change as the impetus to change is the creation of new habits which previous experiences prevent or retard. This ebb and flow propels successive generations who are caught in the habits of historical precedence. To escape habit we have to become conscious of it.

The democratization of the state was intended to dilute power so that a collaborative effort would be required to make the state function; no one person would possess sufficient control to assume it. However, the democratization of the citizenry, especially through the division of labor and extensive consumerism of commodity production has made them utterly powerless giving it a purely rhetorical nature. Yet, and before this, it has always been the effort of the ruling but quiet elite to prevent the democratization of economics (which was essentially the basis for the ratification of the constitution in 1787-88, the unrecognized counter revolution.) In such a scenario the state becomes beholden to capital as its driving force; its interests align with it. It is only in the process of dismantling the present economic structures that it will force the citizenry to assume collective responsibility to drive the state engines willfully in its own interests.

It is not her audience that the artist should concern herself with despite its seemingly practical conveniences. Short term solutions, however, will plague us with long term ruins.

A deconstructed art text begs restructuring - an attempt at elucidating the connections. It is synonymous with the divisions of labor to achieve social needs. But in our present milieu these divisions have also implied divisions in politics and social classes leading to divisions of thought and a tendency to anarchy that is moving towards absolute individualism – their digital pixilation. In this scheme the entrepreneur, then, becomes the structuralist and economics the glue that binds the citizenry socially. There is no monarchy, aristocracy, or nation that it serves. Capital is its own absolute ruler and the entrepreneur his paint brush. We are the deconstructed pieces in this text. However, the artist (proletariat) is not the god of the art text or its financier. She labors for a common purpose - communication - which is the only mechanism to reverse this process.

Habits of thought can be much more sinister than habits of action.

The most important thing that art can teach is the multi-utility of form.

The riddle doesn't change. It is rephrased.

Facts don't just appear. They are the residue of shades created by structures. Facts are the observable phenomenon of structures and obey the rules imposed by structures. They are forensic evidence of their actions. This is applicable to natural phenomenon like the evolution of the biodiversity of our planets as well as within the development of human political, national, social and economic structures. Determining and elucidating the nature of the shadows created by the imposition of various structures on each other requires a dialectic approach. That is why not just a few have harped that the study of history should make it relevant to our present. This is true with any art text. The inability to comprehend this has been mankind's problem that stems from his egoistic nature. Humility and awakening comes when we realize we are just another shadow albeit a special one. We have the ability to discern ourselves.

Many for much of their life search for a Rosetta stone that will help them distinguish false from genuine.

History is often recited with indifference. It needs caring. It needs pain.

If you want to be a poet, you need more than a dexterous tongue.

Habits and not reason determine people's political affiliations. Products are also designed to engender habits. Think about your car.

Misunderstanding the past is dangerous. Cultural traditions naturally require context. But we live in a time where traditions have been abandoned. Mobility, materialism, mass communications have forced their own rituals. This has disconnected us from the past. It's relevance on our present has been disconnected. I don't tote traditions as a social panacea; I imply history, as a study, should be engaged in giving insight into our present motions instead of a version that suits us like a lullaby.

If you want to write don't film. If you want to film learn to speak image. Don't lie with your form. Don't lie in your form.

It is fear of the truth, its implication on our choices that highlights the undercurrent of our contradictions. Rituals, like the surface of the sea, hide these.

The transition to socialism will entail solving the contradictions that capitalism has revealed about man.

Individualism has been capitalism's disease though the basis for its success. Individualism has become an idea for the absolute reduction of human values measured on the broadest commercial-social scale. It defines it as psychology dominating sociology.

A criminal abstraction: a system that demands that your idea of life be connected to its own perpetuation. It makes you an unwitting accomplice.

Self-deception is usually an early character flaw.

Determine if the choices you make are not reactions.

In final analysis content has to control form through a collective choice. It is the only mechanism to man's contradictions. This requires deepening of our collective conscience.

Work is the most real thing anyone can do. Yet it is abstracted and depersonalized. Money becomes its substitute. We need to create jobs and we need to bring worth back into the work. We need to know that our labor has meaning to us and our community. Our work is our community. Everything stems from this.

As fascinating as the psychological development of characters in a novel or cinema can be, the artist that realistically details and creates the social reality of these characters can anchor the psychological attributes to the textual tapestry. Sociology conditions the psychology as its internal logic and movement. It is the ultimate flaw of many books and films today that attempt to fix a modern character into any setting regardless of those settings preconditions. This reflects the contextual priority of determining the content without understanding its relationship to the social aspects most often due to external factors influencing its development. Thus far we have only discussed content. The treatment of the story, how the story is told, is a matter of form. Likewise, in reciprocal and contradictorily fashion, rather than finding new formal means to treat the story, conventions and cliché are used to tell it. Everything is running counter to how it should. Why? When it comes to making money, nothing is ventured. Form is conservatized to a nonsensical story. With such mish mash, nothing can be gained from art.

Don't just remember. Create memories.

NECESSARY

If you're graced

With a long life

Though your mind keen

And your heart still beating

Your body will show you

The corpse it will soon be

But this too is necessary

Truth in intention, in process, in analysis are different yet the same. You are insincere if you ignore what the process asks you to see. Our intentions can bias our analysis if we forego a process that has something to do with discovering the internal contradictions that camouflage our attitudes and beliefs, if we force erroneous processes to validate our intentions and world view. It is being faithful to the process that our intent and ultimately the analysis can help modify our views. We are never masters; only students that attempt to teach others the love for study.

My previous comment on truth stems from the notion that many have confused the idea of an absolute truth and relative truth. Absolute truths are idyllic lapses because process shows us intermediates that would otherwise be ignored. An absolute truth would connect infinite facts into an absolute which is nonsensical.

Process becomes a surrogate substitute of absolute when we remain honest with the conclusions process can shows us.

Don't travel a less traveled road for its own sake.

Reality is the greatest leveler of man despite each and every one of our varied relationship with it.

National boundaries are interesting. Its psycho-social detriments are far reaching. It perpetuates cultural distinctions based on competition. All wars and conflicts are a form of competition.

Class distinctions are rarely the subject of American films and when they do arise they are treated with pixels.

DECEMBER

Individualism is a quixotic adventure.

When you look at a piece of sculpture try to find its motions.

Modern art tries to give poetic sense to the un-poetic.

All real art texts possess a static soul that comes to life when you interact with it purposely.

The current idea of realism has assumed a biased position.

Corporate structures run nations like farmers their cattle and sheep in pens. A little 'bah' isn't going to make the farmer too worried.

Sorrowfully, beautiful has been equated to good. Beautiful is a meaningless concept.

Look for the opposite in art. Every text works with its formal contrast. Identify the obvious then turn it on its head.

Reaching is stretching with purpose.

The social history of art has centered on the relationship of the artist and the benefactor in its most concrete to abstracted aspects. The notion that the artist is free to express is an absurdly idyllic proposition.

Fate: three doors with a prize behind one. Destiny: only one door.

There is nothing more liberating than knowing what you swore to be the truth is false. Your response to that liberation can be joyous or tearful.

The state of balance is an unstable and highly kinetic state. Imbalance is the norm. We pass through balance like a seesaw through its fulcrum.

During a rain fall, if you listen intently, you can recognize the sound of one drop.

Systematically the subjects we can openly discuss are whittled away. Right is right and wrong is wrong dictated by those who can shame us or infringe on our freedoms to work and live. Under the guise of our security we give in and become whittled ourselves. Guernica's occur again and again.

Two dots next to each other make for a very short line.

Three rights make a left the wrong way.

Debt is a valuable commodity to bankers and corporate structures. It functions as a persuasive leveraging tool. All wars attempt to camouflage these facts. In fact, all wars are a product of these tools breaking. Sacrificing your life for such an adventure is naturally delusive. So, patriotism comes in and the fervor of nationalism flames passions and fires. The debt is then resettled. History books are rewritten and stories are told. Debt is accumulated again.

We are addicted to our privileges.

Use the experience offered in an art text to live a second life.

After every revolution the bourgeois parties offer a forum for various constituents to share power in a gesture of amicable solidarity and democratic sensibility. The socialists, representatives of the working classes, must not enter such a constituency with any thought other than subordination of all their work to the certain abduction of the power wrested by the revolution. This amounts to certain betrayal on the part of the socialists.

Content and form in an art text are in a perpetual state of struggle and conflict with each other. This is the pinnacle of the mystery of art.

An art text is an arbitrary system of signs and conventions that the artist attempts to impregnate with sincerity.

Art has its own rules - its systems of checks and balances - that the artist must surrender to despite her nature. A revolution is living art.

Many voices speaking out of turn creates a harsh and deafening dissonance. Working cohesively together with purpose the voices become a melodious coral symphony. The musician/composer, as a leader, has to bring about this harmony in the service of the music she creates. This purpose they then share.

Art is instructive in the affairs of politics. But this kind of leadership has been lacking almost always.

Let the real stir your imagination. It is far more compelling.

The idyllic is not a road that is traveled. It is a mental wandering to pass the time away to your destination. Keep an eye on the hazardous road.

The world is like a large Etch-A-Sketch™. The ghost lines of previous sketches always remain but barely visible in the current drawing.

The only things I own are my experiences. Even my skin I borrow.

Anger can arise out of love or hate. Love is unselfish.

Convenience is becoming an arduous undertaking.

It is allowable to say what happened. But say why it happened ... committing heresy.

TO KNOW A PLACE YOU HAVE TO STAY THERE A WHILE

A few hours or perhaps days

Walking the streets and back alleys

Finding your way

Remembering the grocer who bid you good day

Next to the café you sat to eat breakfast just yesterday

You might have to meander further out

Even linger on the outskirts watching the cars pass

Along distant roads that travel

Beyond furrowed lands where the wheat grows

And the quiet soaks up your thoughts

Maybe a few seasons will be enough

To feel the change in the weather

Transform the colors and hues

Watch the leaves cover the streets

And if you wake up early enough to

Watch the street sweepers clean the roads

And much later in the spring linger on the scent of budding plumes

Breathing the warm breeze that caresses you

You have to sit on a bench on a late summer afternoon

Watching the people take their evening stroll

You have to eavesdrop to see how the boys talk to the girls

How the children come together to play a game of chase the ball

How the old men sit and speak of blissful yesterdays

While the women coyly display their colorful garments

With decorative tinsels

You have to come invited and take part in their festivals

Feel no shyness to sing and dance

Indulge in tasting the foods infused with rich spices

Till your belly aches and the liquor

Makes your head light

And late conversations that give way to bursts of laughter

That echoes in the dark of the night

Long after the bride and groom cried their goodbyes

Maybe a few years to study their language

To laugh at a joke only they would understand

About a neighbor whose wife ran away with another man

To catch the delicate nuances in a few lines of poetry

With genuine tears that catch you unaware

To remember the melody of songs you have listened to so many

times

That now they help you pass into sleep

And on waking you feel

You have always known this place as something that

Has always been part of your heritage.

You have to stay there a little while.

Necessity reduces choice. Creation of political and economic necessity has been the instrument by which all else in our present epoch has followed.

Social paradox: We are taught to compete, but when you compete, whether you win or lose, you lose.

Content is always trapped in form. New content requires escape into and through new forms.

A bird is in the air

Her wings glide as the wind sets her aloft

Dreams watch over her flight

Her horizon is afire when she wakes

Artists don't create new things. They make associations between things that exist that had never been done.

War: achieving peace through violent gluttony. Peace: a state of satiated coma.

A lie can be more revealing than the truth.

The artist struggles with the aesthetics she employs to give shape to the content of her narrative. Form can alter the relativism that exists in the contextual comparison - over emphasizing or under stating. Form distorts for the sake of content or for its own sake (art for art's sake). The lie and truth are contained in one and the same.

Form's aesthetic wanderings must be grounded by content's myopic regard for the facts. The battle between these two has been the cause of insanity in many artists.

Repeating motifs, themes, in films, like in poetry or a melody, leave their impressions like ocean waves that come ashore pulling at your senses as they recede.

"The motion of images, the movement between images; the actor robs cinema its essence." Robert Bresson

Good and bad are relatively meaningless concepts. Selfishness and unselfishness are more precise. Consumerism has made us feel good about our selfish behavior. This has created a pathological state in us. Selfishness breeds apathy. This circumvents democratic necessity for social existence.

All stories regard the issue of a power struggle. Current systemic processes have divorced this direct relationship. Complicity is hidden by process. Narratives in art texts have to connect us back to these seemingly unconnected threads or else we stop learning. Current popular narratives are, in this regard, counterproductive.

Escape from escapism.

Jokes are very effective forms of propaganda.

A photograph of the Mona Lisa is equivalent to a video of an actor reciting a soliloquy. Neither contains the creation of art. They are only reproductions. Reproductions contain no value regardless of the profits assumed by them. Arguably, in the case of the actor, it is a double reproduction, as the art was in the literature.

A photograph, because of its technological factors, does contain evidentiary residue of the truth. However, as a representational crystallization of the moment, it is nothing but a lie. As a formal communication text, as a new experience, it possesses the possibility of explicating the truth. Each of these factors needs to be taken in consideration.

A film crew begins by gathering dirt, straw, gravel and water and mixing the mud then pouring it into rectangular molds ready to be fired into bricks. These bricks are finally hauled into the editing room and piece by piece sorted and fitted into an edifice. Now stands the narrative illusion, whole, and complete.

The left and right hand do not belong to two different people. In concert they work molding and shaping. Who do these democrats and republicans think they really are?

It is easy to hide the lies in rhetoric but hard to hide the truth in action.

Class struggle and national struggle are antagonistic. During working class revolutions the term civil war belies the real struggle taking place. It would be more correct to state it as a class struggle occurring in a nation. The American Civil war, on the other hand, was a bourgeois crisis of the land owners against the industrialists. Its rhetoric of class struggle for the emancipation of the African-American slaves was simply that.

JANUARY

Progress: We are charging it on our children's credit cards.

There is something primal about swimming in the surf. At first we resist the pounding of the waves with exuberance with an infinite sense of resilience. But fatigue sets in and we grow weary our attitudes about this relationship begins to change. We seek the comfort of the sand while we watch our children take on the waves anew.

Words change when you bring other words near them. This is true of colors and musical notes. This is true of culture too.

In a drama which is more tragic a catastrophe or a disappointment?

STOP as a verb is an action word. It is not one human-kind has mastered.

Delineate for yourself the act of creation from reproduction. Reproduction is imitation, an echo, whose quality has shown to garner productive economic value. All our energies are thus channeled through those crevices that reverberate the strongest. In this sense audiences are shaped to respond to loud echoes. The source? What of it if it has no reproductive capacity?

It has been many centuries that the critic has been the guardian of artistic taste and development. Their opinions are waited for both in an artist's determination of their own self-worth and the audiences' attitudes - talk about out sourcing.

The study of art for aesthetic purpose is a lost cause. The study of art in its socially complex communicative structures opens infinite solutions to impasses. All art has been the objective defiance against the impossible.

Not an experience remembered but memory as an experience; Impressionism.

Imagination is certainly one of woman's greatest capacities. But it can often lead to self-delusion.

Actors on stage, actors in movies, actors in life. Actors only in life. Vogue mania. Popularism. But from high in the sky the cities and all the people that live in them appear like a blurred thin cloth, a veil, shivering over the surface of earth.

Ultra materialism - ultra violence.

We have achieved an acute level of relativism in our materialism. It stagnates our intellectual faculties. We abandon them. The crisis of the subconscious has become normal.

Impressionism in art caused the beginnings of form-interpretation. Necessary but a slippery slope if you forget that art is communication and not a medium or an object for aesthetic purpose.

Sample the real in your ideations in art even at the cost of the self's romantic leanings.

Explanations show but don't change a person.

We live on the edge of reality and ideals. Reality shapes our experiences but are expressed through ideals. However, it is the only place we can exist.

The wind that shapes the rocks into spectacular spires is not art.

When our subconscious, our psychological make-up, is fractured, fragmented, isolated, compartmentalized, we fall into in-action. Consumerism has become substituted as a pre-occupation with our in-actions. Consumerism is action externalized from our conscious.

Regardless of our education, status, experiences, all children see the differences between the haves and have not. It sets their life tone.

We don't have awareness of our relationship with our actions. They have become automated.

... And the difference between half-empty and half-full is patience.

What is the riddle of the chicken and the egg but a discussion on form and content?

In the darkest hour remain half-full. Guarded optimism brings solutions and solutions validate optimism.

Those without experience have the strongest opinions.

Incidentally, if you are a North African nation, don't try to start your own bank.

If you have free time ask who made it possible.

The beach is a close knit tapestry of red umbrellas dotted by yellow and blue ones. The sand was buried.

Facts have threads that connect to other facts like lock and key. There is, in the construction of narratives, unlocking the door and entering and there is breaking and entry. Which narrative you wish to choose depends on your method and purpose.

You have to construct the narrative out of facts and not fix the facts to the narrative.

Progress is not iPhone version 5.0. We have yet to define it.

New Year's Resolution 101: Make a non-binding resolution.

Don't return to a place and expect the same experiences. Remembering is simply our way of dealing with the recurrent themes in our lives.

Something to consider: Another crime drama with expected schematic twists? What about using this conventional genre to reflect on the relationship between these two - the cop and robber – and show how structure compels their actions; how one fulfills the other. No, better. Let's remake *Les Miserables*.

Force, politically, is the prime mover. It is from this context geopolitical global action should be re-evaluated.

Be flexible and judicious with your stubbornness but know the limits of your compromise.

"Economic freedom had the same historical roots as political liberalism; both were among the achievements of the enlightenment and were logically inseparable." Arnold Hauser

This remains the contradiction of our era.

Do not relate to me your emotions. I don't want your dramatic interpretations. I am interested in what you have seen. This will compel me to feel.

The GAME aspect of theater that movies have mastered, the ability to pull their audiences into the turns of the plot, has come to dominate all aspects of what we understand movies and films to be. The GAME is not the ART but surely the GAME has compelled a certain acceptance by audiences that makes a discussion on art with audiences seem impenetrable. The real GAME however is the external propaganda, the ideology that exists beyond the text that merges into the entertainment audiences receive. This is certainly cunning.

Real experience in our life is probably equivalent to a pencil line on a big white sheet of paper. Where two lines cross ... that is the stuff of legends.

There is seemingly too much of not enough ... in both cases.

The difference between humans and other animals is that we have learned to accumulate.

Auto-plagiarism; every artist is guilty of it. It is inevitable. We repeat ourselves. We repeat ourselves.

Death, the change in that relationship that experiences it, is a subject most difficult to give a proper accounting.

Things resembling the truth are the pernicious big lies that continue to confound.

A quantum of optimism that is sufficient to pass through the eye of a needle.

What is art but one facet by which we preserve, change and reflect on the state of our culture?

A person invested with authority becomes a channel for action.

Dreams must be subordinate to and in service of reality.

What is the relationship between the violinist and composer? Yes, both have talent. One is an artisan and is a facilitator; reproducer. The other is the artist; creator.

A thousand violinists can play Beethoven's concerto. There is only one Beethoven that lives in the music.

I am more interested in the day after the conclusion of a love story.

Art is not the medium. Art text is not the art. Talent is necessary - to speak a language you have to learn it. But talent does not make an artist. It makes them a craft person. To be an artist your senses have to be open, hard wired to your brain, giving expression to your observation, your thoughts, within the language you choose to express it in. This need to communicate compels you.

You can't be a realist and despair (give up.)

If fundamentally our nature is to have lifelong friendships and relationships with people we love, well, our present economic models are tallying one night stands.

Justice, she should be the honored guest but waits outside her knocking unanswered.

Ugly is also in the eye of the beholder.

We have developed a very acute and selfish idea on issues of fairness.

Negative space is ellipsis. By relying on form you exponentially increase your content. Understanding negative space in your chosen medium is the beginning of the act of creation. Einstein grasped this from a scientific perspective. Art has been accomplishing this for centuries though intuitively.

All art texts begin in negative space. It is never the addition of positive space but the removal of negative space that is actually occurring.

Accolades are fleeting tributes but an intimate conversation can linger a lifetime.

What is important and what we are made to think is important.

The Day and the Dream.

Hollywood movies are very efficient in their story telling. They have parsed it down to the minimum. Their focus is on offering heightened realism that is emotionally charged. You walk away feeling you were in the boxing ring.

The human cost usually falls low on the priority especially for those with little "economic" worth. Such thought is common place in developed countries. In this regard, action is invisible; rhetoric all encompassing.

In current economic discussions the organic components fail to get mentioned; the disconnect is willful.

Watching a movie again and expecting a different ending? The same solutions to the same problems expecting different results. Why not?

Wars confuse reason.

Film techniques create such emotional illusions that the feelings become real. The illusion of the stage begins with accepting it's fake. That initial realization is neglected in cinema. That is its formal power.

The aesthetics of an art text should arise from the precision and economy of the language and not its alluded beauty.

Though the filmstrip moves in one direction, the time schema of a film is expansively fluid.

We are attached to the sense of perpetual detachment. Inundated by constant and rapid stimulus, we have learned to 'let go' to facilitate the next hit which will pass quickly, too. Experiences run through us with the rapidity of Facebook posts. It impacts our world views. Yesterday does not exist. Tomorrow will look like today.

When you LIE, you waste TIME ... geological time.

WE ARE HISTORY

A high tech office built in the room of a gothic church

Skyscrapers rising over subterranean subways built more than a

century ago

New civilizations rising over the ashes of the ancient

A neo-cortex evolving over the reptilian brain

There is no escaping history

We are history

Struggling to remain relevant - you only become obsolete

when you delude yourself.

Ideas formed within your sanctuary are untested.

"Nature and art are two entirely dissimilar phenomena" -

Picasso. With these words he shattered the previous conception of

art since the renaissance.

Experience is the conclusion to the practical application of

ideas.

Why should a painting of a vase of flowers be controversial or instructive? What compels you to select those flowers, cut them, and arrange them in that vase in your home, and then to make them a subject of an artistic rendition, tells me much about you. (Homage to Bresson)

Aesthetics, the persuasive component of the objective prejudice in any art text, can hide that most evident about us.

Economics should be under the strata of culture. But now it determines it.

Narrative is a logical construct (or attempt at it) of the ideas that come to our conscious. Every thought is a reflection of our experiences transformed from the organic into the abstract inter-neuronal connections. The narrative is a detailed echo of the content of this process.

If political action and dialogue make utter nonsense it is because we are too involved in listening to content than to structure. Structural dialogue operates on a different wavelength; political action is the effect left by "the wind cutting its impression into the water."

Every master creates many failures until at the moment of willful creation surprise is unearthed and a masterpiece is born.

FEBRUARY

Must a rhyme repeat itself to become a rhyme?

Current economics is a language of a material world in its impractical applications.

Language is enchained by tradition. It can't be otherwise.

Hero-worship is ideological laziness. It is political laziness.

People may be thrown into positions of power which is understandable. But those that covet power become secretive. This was Stalin.

Boredom is a luxury.

History begins with the realization that there is a tomorrow.

The third dimension in film is time. The spatial element is theater's historic prison enchaining cinema.

Be your own harshest critique. But also show yourself kindness.

Drone surveillance? Is it a political issue? We are surveyed every second. The minuscule details of our lives are analyzed and parsed. Where is the will against such a commercial onslaught? This withered will, against what will it stand? Even the limits of our protests are kept within protestant etiquettes.

Not all perspectives carry the same weight. Consider Carl Sagan's comments below as to the vision of a Europe-centered earth of 500 years ago. Consider this and as well as the current parallels on the issues of perspective as we engage in political, environmental, militaristic and economic suicide:

"Look again at that dot. That's here. That's home. That's us. On it everyone you love, everyone you know, everyone you ever heard of, every human being who ever was, lived out their lives. The aggregate of our joy and suffering, thousands of confident religions, ideologies, and economic doctrines, every hunter and forager, every hero and coward, every creator and destroyer of civilization, every king and peasant, every young couple in love, every mother and father, hopeful child, inventor and explorer, every teacher of morals, every corrupt politician, every "superstar," every "supreme leader," every saint and sinner in the history of our species lived there-on a mote of dust suspended in a sunbeam.

The Earth is a very small stage in a vast cosmic arena. Think of the endless cruelties visited by the inhabitants of one corner of this pixel on the scarcely distinguishable inhabitants of some other corner, how frequent their misunderstandings, how eager they are to kill one another, how fervent their hatreds. Think of the rivers of blood spilled by all those generals and emperors so that, in glory and triumph, they could become the momentary masters of a fraction of a dot.

Our posturing, our imagined self-importance, the delusion that we have some privileged position in the Universe, are challenged by this point of pale light. Our planet is a lonely speck in the great enveloping cosmic dark. In our obscurity, in all this vastness, there is no hint that help will come from elsewhere to save us from ourselves.

The Earth is the only world known so far to harbor life. There is nowhere else, at least in the near future, to which our species could migrate. Visit, yes. Settle, not yet. Like it or not, for the moment the Earth is where we make our stand.

It has been said that astronomy is a humbling and character-building experience. There is perhaps no better demonstration of the folly of human conceits than this distant image of our tiny world. To me, it underscores our responsibility to deal more kindly with one another, and to preserve and cherish the pale blue dot, the only home we've ever known."

— Carl Sagan, *Pale Blue Dot: A Vision of the Human Future in Space*

The new movement in art that was evident in the last century went awry like the receding tide afraid of the daunting task before them. Mysticism, romanticism, hero worship and its siblings now play in the tide pools. The horrific truth, unrelenting penetration, and scathing exposition – these await for the next surge.

The illusion of art is to shatter the illusions.

Drones are cultural icons.

"We are at a stage in human history that is as monumental as changing from a hunter/gatherer society to an agricultural society and from an agricultural society to and industrial society. Where we're headed now will be different because we have exhausted planetary space and human space for us to continue to look at things through the Cartesian measurement of material things. We need to face the way we used the world for our gains, pleasures, and satisfactions. This is the way we evolve to a higher

stage of humanity. And unless we want to live in terror for the rest of our lives, we need to change our view about acquiring things. We have the opportunity to take a great leap forward in these very challenging times. We need to change our institutions and ourselves. We need to seize opportunities. We need to launch our imaginations beyond the thinking of the past. We need to discern who we are and expand on our humanness and sacredness. That's how we change the world, which happens because WE will be the change."

- Dr. Grace Lee Boggs, 93, a long-time Detroit political and labor activist, author, and philosopher.

Greater than God's creation of the universe is man's creation of narrative.

O' crescent moon

The poets sing and recite

Verse to you

With romantic pangs and two-dimensional imagination

We build psychological shells, social shells, institutional shells, material shells, around our fragile ego. We have become an ossified onion with a fart trapped inside.

Some people think I scream because I can't hear ... I can't listen.

Fear begets social silence.

At what point do human mistakes become atrocities?

With pomp and circumstance to the victors has the pen of history belonged. The names of the defeated are simply footnotes.

Humans are filled with contradictions and this is not necessarily revealing. However, as long as these just bend us and not break us we continue with them. It is only surprising how flexible we have become.

Apathy is the source of ... oh, who cares?

If art is MEANINGFUL to you then art IS meaningful to you.

An artist, whether a writer or film maker, if she is interested in asking important questions and finding those answers will have no need to fabricate a narrative out of thin air. Both the story and form of it will evolve out of this pursuit.

An old picture capturing a moment from the past framed behind a piece of glass is itself trapped by the present revealing the chasm between us.

Every action will have a reaction. The issue is are your prepared to understand the cause of that action that should compel a thoughtful response in you. Otherwise a reaction is a reflexive response that further hinders understanding. And consider additionally, you are starting in the middle of it all.

With the renaissance evolved the nefarious Machiavellian political thought that capital has mechanized and automated.

You don't think about breathing but it is the most important thing that you do.

Celebrating your individuality is not the same as condoning a philosophy of individualism.

Your kind and lofty sentiments pass like gas ... Mr. Bush.

Fear and money are strong motivation but not as strong as fearing the loss of money. Everything in current politics is entangled by these two issues.

Tragedy is in the details.

Cinema allows you to rewind. This too is a fresh perspective. No other art allows this.

We fly in our dreams but the gravity of our realities plants our feet to the ground. When these coincide these are often accidental. Rarely ever so, we build a plane.

I scream and scream even though I know I can get more accomplished with a whisper.

Examine your passive conservatism. Your life gives you sufficient time.

Many artists linger in a period when their technique masters them. To master your technique also means mastering yourself. Then and only then, instead of using form to create effect, the effect of your content translates into a form.

The search for a new form is not a trivial matter. Mastery of that form, its final imposition into culture - a historic process - cannot be measured in time but it takes time for its maturation. And then ...

Psychologically, socially, and culturally we remain in a prolonged period of reaction.

Justice is not in the eye of the beholder.

We don't realize that no amount of power can empower us.

When we communicate more than words, more than understanding the words occurs.

Propaganda used to mean the art of telling the truth. Now it means the art of telling a lie with the semblance of a truth.

There are no powerful words. But there have been powerful people with many words.

Commercials are propaganda that works. That's why politicians speak sound bites.

Patriotism and nationalism are intimately and seductively tied to consumerism. Challenge this paradigm and you are an outcast. With a significant but disturbing logic I have to admit that real environmentalism is un-American. Even the word environment has taken on the most commercial attitude.

Understanding someone doesn't require that you speak their language. It can be effortless.

The multiple of art forms, the varied approaches, the multitude of means, speaks to our wealth of material. Why is our philosophy so impoverished?

Ask not what the world can do for you; ask what you can collectively do for the world. J.F.K. needed to take it up one more level.

"Extraordinary claims require extraordinary evidence."— Carl Sagan

The issue isn't one of faith or disbelief. Like buildings and cities, we, as people, are living history though the threads of our collective cultures and traditions are lost and forgotten. The building too stands with the footprints of the ages passing through its corridors accumulating the residue.

We need collective encouragement.

We are taught history by periods and dates and events. How meaningless and unjust.

Art is influenced and influences. The continuity in historical processes also exists across disciplines. When these disciplines take on an independent character they begin to create internal contradictions as they forget their part in a broader social dialogue that is continuous and ongoing.

A finished tangible product becomes the most abstract thing created.

Artistic forms have all existed essentially unchanged in our known history. How these forms become employed, what the artists want to say and how they say it, undergo linguistic modifications as our psychology interacts with evolving social movements. Oftentimes the contradictions that exist between psychology and social forces compel the text's context.

We all start in the middle of a circle searching for the beginning as an end to its mean.

Artistic content does not obey the laws of thermodynamics.

New forms evolve in an attempt to give expression to unexpressed or inexpressible content. It is from this sense that form creates content. Form comes out of the need to give expression created by new social relationships that are constantly developing.

Form is an extremely conservative matter. This does not mean it can't give expression to truly revolutionary events.

Knowing is a tricky concept. It is also embracing its opposite.

Be cognizant of how much all the people around you do that makes it possible for you to do.

Art texts acquire historically mediated external baggage. There is no way to read Hamlet outside of our own context.

ON THE GOLF COURSE

The puttering of a distant lawn mower

Manicuring the putting greens before sunrise

A dim headlight guides the way

For the eyes hidden behind the darkness

It is only through subjectivity that objectivity is perceived.

History seems to be showing us that progress is slower than evolution.

Fish don't feel 'wet.'

When you know your barista's cousin's name you have a serious coffee addiction.

Hope is eternal if you are honest, sincere, altruistic and principled. That's not too much?

Be wary of political entertainment.

Harder than pushing a mountain is pushing the wind.

Violence is a learned behavior. So is condoning it. What we haven't realized are its different levels and qualities.

Though our lives are continuous it is selectively edited.

If a text is really a tragedy it is because the issues within the narrative are important. The striving is important. The chasm between the idea and the limits to its practical application creates the tragic. The striving reflects the best in us.

We discovered a few centuries ago, under the weight of evidence, that the earth was not the center of the universe. But we continue to believe man is.

The weight of limitless time is counterpoised by man's limitless arrogance.

It is difficult to explain things that aren't felt beforehand.

Sometimes utopic dreams and offerings arise from lack of experience with new structures. From this construct it remains a truism that content can only follow form.

MARCH

"The struggle itself [...] is enough to fill a man's heart. One must imagine Sisyphus happy." Albert Camus

If you take away Sisyphus' rock, you take away Sisyphus.

The study of history is the rendition of the past shaped into a version that attempts to fit the known facts. The implication of those facts, what they mean, and how the meta-facts fit into the ongoing narrative, are the challenges faced by the historian. However, regardless of his impartiality, the historian is a thread within the tapestry he weaves. His ability to see is conditioned within this web.

Know the limits of psycho-analysis. It is a dangerous tool in hands ill or too adept at it.

Be aware that in your position on issues that the content of your arguments should attempt to bring the context and structure of the process into awareness. Otherwise little is accomplished. There is nothing gained by marring a person or situation when there is no clear context for it. Again, and always, historical dialectics gives context to the interrelationships of countries and their present stands.

You can be very smart, a genius, utterly brilliant and commit banalities. If you can take constructive criticism you will persevere. If you are arrogant and self-serving or self-indulgent then you have more than a few mountains still to climb.

The night after a novel, a painting, a piece of music has been completed, after the artist slumbers, the piece quietly cuts loose and gains its independence from its creator. It germinates and flowers set adrift on its own momentum. The artist and the piece diverge.

The competition in our lives is relentless.

Tragedies of life are not the same ones as artistic tragedies.

Art has the capacity to confront life instead of be paralyzed by it.

Art texts as facilitators – an idea, germinal, hidden but present, can identify for the future their incomprehensible. Art texts offer new experiences for life.

Is it Shakespeare for Shakespeare's sake or because his characters, flawed and disfigured as they are, opened chasms deep into our own psychology?

Editing is the highest mental function we possess. Every discipline uses it.

Broken schools trying to medicalize behavior: The standard deviation on the accepted mean is extremely narrow and defined by quack psychiatrists and by overworked teachers needing to perform under arbitrary standards whose measures are meaningless and harmful. Children navigate a complex social structure with blindfolds. Rigidity leads to pathology.

Laws do two things: secure life/people and secure property. This has merged implicitly into securing the rights of people with property. The study of economics has arisen to give defense to this contradiction.

There is no word in classical economics on social justice. A discipline confined to its internal metrics, as important as economics is, cannot explain its actions or contradictions.

Nostalgia can be dangerous. So much of politics, movements in entertainment, and the socially disgruntled exalt it. It is a decadent behavior; an inability to see beyond the obvious.

Data is a branch from a tree that will hang you or rescue you.

Our individuality has been homogenized and then atomized. In a consumer society this atomization is important for marketing and selling. Standardizing makes the process efficient and controllable. It applies to political processes. Selling products and buying votes are not dissimilar. But it is also important to know we are the commodity and not the material (i.e. iPhone) being sold. We, collectively, are being manufactured. (See Noam Chomsky)

Every slogan seeks confirmation in action. However, action is conditioned by external circumstances. Like a blossoming seed action also depends on the season, the fertility of that soil, and proper cultivation of the fruits. However, we live in an environment filled with Monsanto slogans.

Fiction is a facilitator.

People have always had relationships with inanimate objects; heirlooms, homes, books, paintings. But our involvement with our devices borders on a love affair. They are alive.

We are cultural addicts of technology - not one that betters our life but encumbers it.

People severely underestimate the authority and influence the media has on shaping consent and giving legitimacy to ideology and its scope. Liberals and conservatives alike operate under a rigid narrow purview.

Democracy should own national security otherwise democracy becomes meaninglessly shackled as it is. This is a civic responsibility. The legal issues behind these are democratic issues as well.

Your transformative capacity lies not in belief as much as resolve to know the complex interrelationships between disparities in the presented facts. The premise always begins with principles; a set of codes that need to be tested and proved or discarded. "I believe" is fraught with havoc and compromise.

Some people are scared of heights. Others are scared of happiness. These are not so different.

There shouldn't be any task beneath a doctor in service to the patient.

It is important that once in our life we learn and feel real love as well as real grief and that these mold the substance of our character towards a constructive social purpose whatever this purpose may be.

[The study of] History is a spotlight to the distant darkness.

God and Satan; Absolute and relative; Concrete and abstract; Love and like; Tarzan and Jane; Obama and Bush;

Carnegie and Mother Teresa; Confucius and confusion; War and peace; Crime and punishment. More war. That's it. More war.

We live on the fringes of reality. All our positions on issues stem from the ridiculous circus constructed around our excesses.

It isn't that we see different facts. We are blind to their cause.

When you are in a quiet space the loudness in the distance becomes sharper. This is true of light also and true of moral fortitude. As the din of the ambient noises (those of mainstream media and all the incessant events of this and that) reaches a crescendo we filter and inhibit our senses instead of absorb and heighten them.

The truth is always revealed when it becomes irrelevant. This fact is always concealed from the present.

I never get tired of seeing the GREEN in vegetation nor the deep BLUE in the sky. Even the SILVER in the clouds shimmers with glee.

A real historian knows each ingredient in the soup of facts, how they were treated, and why.

Leaders should be the conduits for the masses a reflection of an awakened consciousness. This brain needs to address the total organism. However, we listen too much to our stomach.

An actor that shows you hunger is perhaps a competent actor. But this does not make it great cinema. The actor, as a valuable commodity, has become a crutch to the director rather than putty to be formed for its material properties. This, you may say, is the reality, but how fatalistic.

We balance individual with societal needs. Our psychological make-up is an unusual dynamic mixture of these forces. Social characteristics are a generalization of the average of the individual psychological personalities of its citizenry.

There is in every artist a strong element of fake. It is to the purpose of that fake that distinguishes them from each other.

Don't dig your own grave, grave digger.

"The production of a real work of art requires the presence of a sound and cautious mind with roots in living cultural tradition and command of a stock of practicable devices, a capacity to learn and to assimilate, a readiness to experiment, to delete, and to start again." Arnold Hauser

Terminal exhaustion - when every oxygen molecule is scavenged.

"It may be said that the will of the working masses of the whole of the civilized world, directly influenced by the course of events, is at the present moment incomparably more revolutionary

than their consciousness, which is still dominated by the prejudices of parliamentarism and compromise." Trotsky from *Terrorism and Communism*

"In such conditions, the presence of a revolutionary party, which renders to itself a clear account of the motive forces of the present epoch, and understands the exceptional role amongst them of a revolutionary class; which knows its inexhaustible, but unrevealed, powers; which believes in that class and believes in itself; which knows the power of revolutionary method in an epoch of instability of all social relations; which is ready to employ that method and carry it through to the end – the presence of such a party represents a factor of incalculable historical importance." Trotsky from *Terrorism and Communism*

Nationalism is the sine qua none of the usurpation of proletariat conscious away from the class struggle to the imposition and acceptance of imperial demagoguery. It functions to redirect true class contradictions imposed by the encompassing social superstructure driven by its economic directives to the erroneous conception of a national struggle for self-identity and preservation. It is a diverting strategy. This is not a new idea. It has been reiterated and addressed on numerous occasions but remains difficult to surpass as current laws and political structures, the media blitzkrieg, and general economic underpinnings avoid redirecting the discussion unto real issues that cause so much of our suffering.

By example, what is Netanyahu's and western powers current controversy with Iran but a smoke screen to deter from the real terrorism and prejudices imposed by Zionism over the Palestinians? (See Miko Peled) The proletariat must recognize that its ambitions aren't the same as those currently in power. Rather than desiring what the haves have, they have to redirect their efforts to reconceptualizing what societal and human needs dictate.

The dilemma of a two state solution: If you (Israel) deny a people (Palestinians) equal legal rights to the same land you both occupy then it is easy to legally dispense with their human rights by creating false borders and then sounding the drum beats of perpetual war.

You are born with two eyes - one that focuses on the details and the other one that looks out on the horizon. With your one brain process these simultaneously.

We are all essentially prisoners of life.

These are the "words" history has given us. These are the ones we use. No other.

The first counter-ideological charge by the status quo against alternative solutions is UTOPIAN ILLUSIONS.

Our personal movements are from group to group. Groups give us confidence and a sense of identity. The motion away (exclusion from the group by the group or personal choice) robs us of this. We feel isolated and outside. Group influence can be profound and necessary. It is for this reason open criticism and free dialogue must be maintained and insisted upon to counter both oppressive directions - subjection and isolation. It is how our individuality manifests itself in this inter-communicative process.

Rationalization is a method of distorting (the facts). They are manipulated into and for a subjective-objective. The fragments edited out contain much relevant information. (PSYCHOLOGY)

In the case of wars they are attempts against revolution in favor of stasis.

Tensions are created by the motions towards and away. Watch these relativistically.

STYLE: Trends are historically tied. They are the cement in the edifice of content and form. It is the concrete expression of an internalized psychology within an external social process.

STYLE: What compels me to draw or write like I do? It's like a hidden mirror, a reflection of my personality revealed to myself. It is a stranger to me on hearing my own voice for the first time. It is me but not quite as I think of myself. I am exposed to myself and, yes, they are my flaws revealed. But they are a constant; the expression of my social self.

STYLE: It is the residue of the complete internal artistic process externalized. It functions in the psychological and social realm and, so, possesses a history or past tense that is both personal/internal and objective/external yet an entity completely relegated to FORM. For these reasons it remains difficult to forensically examine.

PARADOX: Hide that which you want people to see. (It is rule number one in cinema.) - Paraphrasing Bresson

"Whereas the late King James the Second by the Assistance of diverse evill Councellors Judges and Ministers employed by him did endeavour to subvert and extirpate the Protestant Religion and the Lawes and Liberties of this Kingdome (list of grievances including) ... by causing several ...good Subjects being Protestants to be disarmed at the same time when Papists

were both Armed and Employed contrary to Law, (Recital regarding the change of monarch) ... thereupon the said Lords Spiritual and Temporall and Commons pursuant to their respective Letters and Elections being now assembled in a full and free Representative of this Nation taking into their most serious Consideration the best meanes for attaining the Ends aforesaid Doe in the first place (as their Ancestors in like Case have usually done) for the Vindicating and Asserting their ancient Rights and Liberties, Declare (list of rights including) ... That the Subjects which are Protestants may have Arms for their Defense suitable to their Conditions and as allowed by Law." EXCERPT FROM THE ENGLISH BILL OF RIGHTS 1689 which was the basis for the 2nd Amendment of the US Bill of Rights:

Where is the King today?

A paradox is not the same as a contradiction. Open to one and blind to the other.

We live only on one page - the one that is being written and read simultaneously. The previous ones are left to our clouded memories. When the page is turned the story, our part in it, will end and will be forwarded to them that will stand on their page to make sense of this long winded but not very forgiving or compassionate story of human existence to make sense of and decipher.

Economic thinking, when this is the main outlook on life, all other facets atrophy. Compassion and cooperative rationales come to make little sense.

Economics is not physics. It is currently an excuse.

Deviant thought has often been cloaked into mainstream norms. Being GAY isn't deviant. Thinking that BEING GAY IS DEVIANT is deviant. And tying procreation to marriage is simply absurd. Marriage as a historical institution was tied to seeing women as property. Marriage needs redefining to emphasize equity and equality foremost; and its very personal nature which speaks to personal freedoms.

Competition is but only one method of many to motivation but it is the basest. Neither free trade advocates, nor the libertarians, and neither the Keynesians have given a comprehensive or honest examination of this issue. It is the hornet's nest.

ECONOMICS: from the Greek, *oikonomikos* - household management. Not household wrecking.

The painter that burns his completed canvas before any other eye has set their sight upon it has said nothing.

Perhaps you begin to consider not taking anymore. But then you see another does take. Then another and another and you find yourself feeling anxious. Now you consider undoing your consideration.

A very good friend knows when to walk away from you.

Politics is the crashing wave and economics the undertow.

Why now do the media harp on the lies of the Iraq war long after the graves of the dead are forgotten? This too is a distraction.

There can be more political truth in the pen of a mediocre artist than all the hot air in congress.

When seeing a photograph or film, you have to separate the actual from the now fictitious.

Don't lose the poetry in politics and always remain political in your poetry.

A closed ended analysis is a lie.

What are we good at? Compartmentalizing? It is a very troubling defense mechanism.

A smile, a frown, knitted brows, a smirk, a stiff chin. Our experiences create emotions and find expression through our facial responses which become synonymous with conventions that mean happy, sad, worried, irritated or resolved. However these emotions begin inside and aren't borne on our sleeves. Yet, we play with emotions for their own sake in every facet of our communicative endeavors. Movement of emotions becomes more important than ideas. Why?

Conjectures have been a significant part of our "evolutionary" political history. Facts, then, are by such measures revolutionary. But because our cultures have been mostly based on such conjectures traditions/habits have been hard to break. They have wielded a stronger hold on us. We are inherently all conservative regardless of our political opinions. Facts, accepting their influence on us, are the only way forward.

A public shift, a political shift, has engrained itself in nearly every facet of our dialogue since 9/11/2001. Preemption of jurisprudence has become the new normal. Vilification, falsification, and disregards for human rights, has loitered insolently in this place.

Don't be disenchanted with a rose's thorns.

Children; sweet is seeing the sudden sensation of tendrils of cool young grass against the soles of their bare feet. Sweeter is their giggles.

A theory of historic simultaneity: We carve out time and space and within that mental microcosm we attempt to conceptualize the world. Our brains certainly more than just an organ for reflection of the real yet it can only process that time and space that it has mentally conceived. This implies a simultaneous historic totality that it cannot conceptualize or in plain words history is not time dependent.

What woman has created man has stolen.

Form is content's parent though content gave birth to form.

A ripe tomato and flakes of sea salt.

APRIL

Privilege or equality ... M.L.K. understood this but many in the civil rights movement had not.

Austerity isn't just an economic issue. Our civil rights have been curtailed through an insidious process that allows a broader state of exceptions to our rights and capacities. (See the bill of rights; the 1st, 5th, 6th and 8th amendments with regards to recent issues in the news.) In this context, a living constitution becomes just poetic phrases.

Try explaining Hiroshima and Nagasaki.

There stand two tall buildings before us with only a sliver of sky visible between them. But you assert that we have access to seemingly infinite data. There are perhaps millions of books to choose from. The Internet offers videos, pictures, and articles to digest that are endless in quantity. Yet, without acknowledging that that sliver of sky is the view afforded us of our world, one shaped by the imposition of those structures, we can't begin to have a dialogue.

We go to the movies to see performances. The talent is the centerpiece around which the movie is constructed. The shots, the angles, are all shaped by and to enhance the performances. Even the script is written for said talent. And, without batting an eye, the NY liberal elites pander to this Hollywood magic. They have emphatically misunderstood cinema, cheapened theater and remain oblivious to their erroneous opinions. They accept the present state of affairs as fixed. They can't rise beyond their linear thinking to consider the functions of art within the discipline of communication. The young fanatic's worship of Star Wars has more merit for me than their critical miss opinions.

Impose democracy on the fields of art. Not on an art text.

There was a video of a man standing on a deserted beach as the tsunami wave hurled at him. He remained motionless until disappearing into the massive wall of water. Our communities and people sit still watching the austerity tsunami hurling into us.

Tasting food can wrest you back into the recess of your clouded memories and experience them with vivid clarity.

Once an (artistic) solution is found it quickly acquires inertia. For the artist it becomes only a brief resting place.

A few know what they want. Most know what they don't want and spend considerable effort and time eliminating them untill ...

Don't just reach deep into your discipline, reach across into other disciplines. The variety in perspectives will triangulate the truth. (And no one discipline is better than another.)

Let us forget, for the moment, that cinema is a unique art form (an idea which came years after it had been "invented" and converted into a business with the face of its stars used to sell dreams.) Somewhat backward but it left the indelible impression that cinema was a vehicle for the reproduction of theatre. Is it a surprise today that those people that call themselves filmmakers and the TALENT approach the construction of filmic texts like a theatrical production using all the nomenclature of the theatre? Not one of them stops to define cinema, to define its art. Every artistic text ultimately becomes an artistic dilemma to solve. It is finding those solutions that give, in the case of our present discussion, a cinematic representation to the purpose of the text. Reproduction, as in the case of recording the theatrical production, is essentially easy. It is laziness disguised as popularity and box office success if these terms have meaning. Cinematic solutions don't come easy. It forces abandoning conventions in search of new formal solutions.

In this sense the actor is the most conventional factor in the cinematic text. They don't contribute. They detract.

We deeply believe in choice but we don't have much choice when the choice we are offered is tied to our starvation.

Jose Lutzenberger: *"He was Brazil's first internationally known environmental activist, and the fact he was chosen environment minister in Brazil's first democratically elected government in 30 years was just a Spiderman indication of the tremendous mark he made in that area,"* said Stephan Schwartzman, senior scientist at Environmental Defense. Lutzenberger's time as the Secretary of the Environment came to an abrupt end. In December 1991, "L. Summers, who at the time was chief economist and a vice-president of the World Bank (later to become President Clinton's Secretary of the Treasury, Harvard President and then chief economic adviser to Obama), made an internal note (leaked to the environmental community) that asserted that the economically correct policy for the disposal of environmental poisons was to dump them in developing countries. Lutzenberger wrote to Summers expressing very strong disapproval of these ideas (calling them 'totally insane'), and was removed from his post immediately thereafter."

[The internal note is copied hereunder]

DATE: December 12, 1991

TO: Distribution

FR: Lawrence H. Summers

Subject: GEP

'Dirty' Industries: Just between you and me, shouldn't the World Bank be encouraging MORE migration of the dirty industries to the LDCs [Least Developed Countries]? I can think of three reasons:

1) The measurements of the costs of health impairing pollution depends on the foregone earnings from increased morbidity and mortality. From this point of view a given amount of health impairing pollution should be done in the country with the lowest cost, which will be the country with the lowest wages. I think the economic logic behind dumping a load of toxic waste in the lowest wage country is impeccable and we should face up to that.

2) The costs of pollution are likely to be non-linear as the initial

increments of pollution probably have very low cost. I've always thought that under-populated countries in Africa are vastly UNDER-polluted; their air quality is probably vastly inefficiently low compared to Los Angeles or Mexico City. Only the lamentable facts that so much pollution is generated by non-tradable industries (transport, electrical generation) and that the unit transport costs of solid waste are so high prevent world welfare enhancing trade in air pollution and waste.

3) The demand for a clean environment for aesthetic and health reasons is likely to have very high income elasticity. The concern over an agent that causes a one in a million change in the odds of prostrate[sic] cancer is obviously going to be much higher in a country where people survive to get prostrate[sic] cancer than in a country where under 5 mortality is 200 per thousand. Also, much of the concern over industrial atmosphere discharge is about visibility impairing particulates. These discharges may have very little direct health impact. Clearly trade in goods that embody aesthetic pollution concerns could be welfare enhancing. While production is mobile the consumption of pretty air is a non-tradable.

The problem with the arguments against all of these proposals for more pollution in LDCs (intrinsic rights to certain goods, moral reasons, social concerns, lack of adequate markets, etc.) could be turned around and used more or less effectively against every Bank proposal for liberalization.

—Lawrence Summers

Euphemisms are aplenty but the end result is not only to dupe the sheep but to make the powerful feel mag·nan·i·mous. Naturally this occurs through their apologists - their public relations people. It is like a cocktail party with all sorts of manners that give it social status and credibility. These are the real ACTORS that deserve the OSCARS. Begin chipping at this facade and they will begin gnashing their teeth.

One must understand what an actor is, what his profession is, his playing. First, the actor never stops playing. Playing is a projection ... That is his movement: he projects himself outside. While your non-actor character must be absolutely closed, like a container with a lid. Closed. And that, the actor cannot do, or, if he does it, at that moment he is no longer anything. For there are actors who try, yes. But when the actor simplifies himself, he is even more false than when he is the actor, when he plays. For we are not simple. We are extremely complex. And it is this complexity that you find with the non-actor ... because he [the actor] had acquired the habit of being an actor to such a degree, even in life, he is an actor. He cannot be otherwise. Live otherwise. He cannot exist otherwise, than exteriorizing himself. – Robert Bresson in interview with Jean-Luc Godard and Michel Delahaye

War ... what good have you ever brought? They seem always to celebrate your entrance and mourn later your devastation only to soon forget again. They are calling your name once more. The spit is roasting succulent meat.

CANNIBALIZATION: Sequestration is not a new concept. The structural adjustments (SA) imposed on the third world nations (Latin, south Americas, Asia, etc.) in the 1970-80's during the evolving Thatcher-Reagan eras utilizing the World Bank and IMF organizations left them powerless, ravaged, and indebted.

Globalization and Free-Markets, our Bermuda short wearing and pudgy uncle and auntie, have returned from their long trips abroad and are now knocking on our door. The issue is not as superficially envisioned by the republicans and democrats as a means to pay down the (war) debt and assume fiscal responsibility for our exuberant spending (which was a massive transfer of wealth to corporate structures.) The people never caused the debt. In other words, the Sequester is the U.S. version of SA to privatize all functions of government. Government, when functioning properly, has legitimate constructive functions for the people but is often seen as a regenerating source for the accumulation of wealth by corporate rationalists. Privatization, as a buyout method, usurps all these necessary functions because of market principles that see people as wealth-generating-commodities. The markets want to take over these as new sources for direct revenue but the cost will be that people will have no real recourse for their own defense as the structure of government will have fundamentally changed.

Fast food workers in New York, you deserve a living wage and more. It belongs to you. Begin teaching what we have forgotten.

See the interface between an object and its surroundings. These illusions of light and lines also impact social movements and the underpinnings of mainstream ideology. Context matters because context plays you foremost as a representation of that interface.

In painting, what is foreground but a ruse to cajole, entice, and woo you into the distant details of the background?

May reason be more than a retrospective exercise?

The republican-democrats' efforts to reduce debt are essentially a measure to privatize all government functions that give social value. The social security coffers are ripe for their picking. They offer no substantive infrastructure building initiatives despite their seething rhetoric against one another. This is the beginning of the magic show.

Actual tangible wealth - Two pigs, cattle, parcel of farm land - is difficult to accumulate while debt is an imaginary construct that is easy to calculate immediate compound interest on. Currently, we exchange debt as our main economic transactions. As imaginary as it is, it has a tremendous stranglehold on people. The current economic maladies in the world are related to debt creation. Nations have been made prisoners to it. Commodity economics is laughable in this context.

Spring begins with the hint of tiny green buds on swaying naked branches at the break of dawn.

We also learn from the things we aren't exposed to.

What we register to be history are those facts caught out of a sea called the past. He who has a boat brings back the catch.

History repeats itself (or rhymes) because we consistently make the same thoughtless and careless mistakes. We choose to give the same interpretation to the disparity in facts.

All meta-facts are the interpretation (subjective) of the material (objective).

History is always running ahead of us.

The cup isn't half empty or full. I'm half thirsty or quenched.

Don't ask an artist why they did what they did. Their response is useless and if one does come it is simply contrived to send the questioner away with their nonsense. What prompted them at a specific moment to choose a phrase, connect images, choose this and not that ... I think the rationale for the choices in details are lost to them. At that moment they felt this or that way. They extracted it ... out of themselves with heroically focused automation and threw it on the canvas only afraid the spell would be broken before they completed their endeavors. At that moment it made sense. These moments are like real dreams forgotten after they woke up and had coffee and heard the distractions of the traffic outside. It is there on the canvas remaining even a mystery to them.

Every 100 years we have a moment of peace. War is the normal state.

Normal is a collective phenomenon.

Hate is a reaction. Disdain is premeditated.

Upon arriving to every problem - an impasse; after departing from every problem - a weigh point of alternative solutions.

Prosaic injustice...

You can name a child angel but the name and disposition aren't necessarily linked. This is true of states that call themselves a democracy.

One of the hardest things to do is describe or draw what you see. There is an immediate subjective interpretation. It takes training to detach ... the 'you.'

Whether you read a book, look at a painting or watch a film, leave your expectations and prejudice at home. Approach the experience of it in a blank slate.

Relatively speaking, the CAMERA eye sees the real world in concrete IMAGES. WORDS, on the other hand, are by definition abstract and are therefore conventionalized and given predefined meaning. Literature's abstraction always begins external to us while the images in cinema, borrowed from real life, the ABSTRACTION begins between the CONCRETE images. It is the mental process that looks for a connection between them. In CINEMA the ABSTRACTION is internal to us and therefore often times missed. The inability to see between IMAGES causes many filmmakers to rely on literature to fill in the missing aspects of their narrative. However, the art of CINEMA depends on NEGATIVE SPACE - the interplay between what is and what is not shown. It is for this reason the ACTOR as a LITERARY facilitator has no place in cinema while the ACTOR as an IMAGE/MODEL is so important to it.

The first person perspective is nearly impossible to sustain in cinema. The eyes of the camera are not the eyes of the character; the voice over narration and intimacy created with the main character substitutes for this. These are conventions. (See: *Diary of a Country Priest* by Robert Bresson)

Just because everything is possible in cinema doesn't mean everything should be possible in cinema.

Hollywood is to film what Monsanto is to seed.

Real and perpetual violence doesn't desensitize you to it. It is a constant reminder and gnaws at you. There is no forgetting it. But when glamorized and beautified, kept distant, then you lose perspective. Even well-meaning journalists don't know when they stick their foot in their mouth.

Journalists often reveal more about themselves than the stories they write about. Borrowed from *The Passenger* by Antonioni

All (political) lies are two lies; the deceit and your consent.

EMOTIONS: a walk on a beach and you find a half buried bottle - This may conjure a story. Sunsets and their colors evoke a sense of warmth and closure. A comedy act - a pie in the face, a slip on a banana - can make you laugh. A knife through a slice of onion can evoke tears. One is an emotion of imagination and the other of experience. The other is calculated for its effect. One is thoroughly a chemical reaction. None of these are artistic nor can be categorized in defining the emotional factors that take place in an art text.

The most effective lie is that the one telling it also believes it. In such a case the ACTOR is the best agent. They live it.

I believe that when someone believes in their own lies they are using complex defense mechanisms to insulate themselves from any pangs of conscience. However, not knowing the truth is not the same as telling a lie. Most people fit in this category. They want to tell the truth and are sincere.

Each potential new species must undergo a genetic revolution. It succeeds or does not. Presently we are functioning at a conscious level.

Religion wasn't invented to give an answer to man's origin. It was invented to give an answer the mystery of man's consciousness.

Romanticism, as a movement, is regressive. It is pathological. It cannot conceive the necessary solutions because it neglects the problem. (It is the problem.) Yet we are living through a significant romantic period in our history. All is theater.

A good argument does not make it true. A self-contained thought needs impact with other thoughts. In the wreckage the shadow of the truth can be discerned ... oftentimes only long after the accident has been cleared of the debris left behind.

Terrorists are essentially cowards. Whatever their cause it is no longer our cause. Whatever their truth they relinquish any moral standing on. They are unprincipled and lack conviction towards any appeal for a humane pursuit. But we also cautiously assert that as we object to and condemn unjust (imperial) wars as crimes, tortures as crimes, the displacement of people from their land as crimes of terror, the brutal actions of militaries acting under false legal national apparatuses (terrorism as national security) for the enrichment of an elite oligarchy while engendering unfounded fear and prejudice in the citizenry, terrorist acts can be counted in this dung heap of maladies. Structurally they work in concert even though theirs is a reaction to a cardinal terrorism.

When will we stop using the term American Indians? They are not Americans as they have been living here far longer than the naming of the country. They are not Indians. That is not their culture. Their regional diversity and tribal cultural differences is tremendous and richer than we have ever given credit to. However, our errors persist. We have given them an identity that is not theirs and stolen from them what is.

The balance of political power at any given moment is determined under the influence of fundamental and secondary factors of differing degrees of effectiveness, and only in its most fundamental quality is it determined by the stage of the development of production. The social structure of a people is extraordinarily behind the development of its productive forces. The lower middle classes, and particularly the peasantry, retain their existence long after their economic methods have been made obsolete, and have been condemned, by the technical development of the productive powers of society. The consciousness of the masses, in its turn, is extraordinarily behind the development of their social relations, the consciousness of the old Socialist parties is a whole epoch behind the state of mind of the masses, and the consciousness of the old parliamentary and trade union leaders, more reactionary than the consciousness of their party, represents a petrified mass which history has been unable hitherto either to digest or reject. Trotsky

The practical aspects of economy are most reliant on the real and raw facts. All our current progress has so far been to this cause. Our social development, lagging, has not assumed a forward position with respect to it.

The political worshipers of routine, incapable of surveying the historical process in its complexity, in its internal clashes and contradictions, imagined to themselves that history was preparing the way for the Socialist order simultaneously and systematically on all sides, so that concentration of production and the development of a Communist morality in the producer and the consumer mature simultaneously with the electric plough and a parliamentary majority. Hence the purely mechanical attitude towards parliamentarism, which, in the eyes of the majority of the statesmen of the Second International, indicated the degree to which society was prepared for Socialism as accurately as the manometer, indicates the pressure of steam. Yet there is nothing more senseless than this mechanized representation of the development of social relations. Trotsky

A socialist must tread cautiously through the capitalist landscape. Its influences can begin shaping his rightward shift unbeknownst to himself. It occurs when his ideals become ossified against the historical developments. Isn't this ultimately the same error?

Parliamentary democracies were intended as crude measures of the constituents' preferences. However, given congresses ratings and the general mismatch in public polls and current political agendas nothing can be further from these idyllic offerings. In such realities democracies operate as particular "dictatorships" from a FORM based analysis. What needs answering is who is dictating and how do they circumnavigate the process? However, parliamentary democracies also engender passivity through "legal niceties" in their constituents. The answer to these questions becomes irrelevant to them yet it is precisely this that needs their utmost attention.

The fundamental error in the defense of capitalism has been to equate it to natural law. This is beyond absurd.

Still waters can stimulate cerebral kinetics.

I think, therefore I am. By extension, we communicate, therefore we are.

Misplaced compromise can be cruel. It is usually the imposition of structure on procedural proceedings. The regressive impact of structure on cultural attitudes is insidious and methodically slow as to be unnoticed. Contradictions in outcomes echo these.

Reality is the wrench thrown into in the well-oiled machinery of your ideals.

Rearranging is not changing.

FAR

You don't have to go up very far to see the curvature on the

horizon

You don't have to go up far to begin losing the minute details

below

You don't have to go up far at all to realize the stars might as well

be figments of your imagination

You don't have to go up far to feel the anguish of catching your

breath for lack of oxygen

You don't have to go far at all to meet another person like you

We are often conscious of what is evident through unconsciously negating the opposite or negative. Contemplate the nature of a king. From the king's perspective there is only the opposite.

What hinders all this discussion becomes the retrospective nature of our dialogue.

MAY

We have for too long associated a romantic attitude to the business of war.

Every mighty nation has had the allegiance of its army. Every mighty nation that fell grew to depend on that allegiance.

There are 20 news personalities clambering over each other to deliver the same breaking news while context is supplied by their hired experts.

Generals make poor poets.

The working classes have been bourgeoisified into believing their dreams of plenty have merit. Solidarity has been made irrelevant.

At the start of the institution of Christianity, around 300 A.D., for it to succeed, they made god intangible and amorphous. Now they make him palpable and personal. However, it is death that connects both of these attitudes and there is no back door to escaping it. These are the religious trappings they offer to life.

Libertarianism is about a hundred years behind corporatism. Ayn Rand, as their queen, espoused a Nietzschean superman concept of individualism and natural rights. Their militarism and nationalism has more in common with fascism than the libertarians want to admit or consider but they remain only a reaction to corporatism. These tendencies are becoming very evident in the social fabrics of current western structures. Again, it isn't an issue of the well-argued ideology but the real implications and structural movements of their ideas set into practice that sends a chill up the spine.

Rarely if ever is there an objective adjective.

Montage narrates structure/form. It offers an alternative content. It comments on, emphasizes, colors and hides, the obvious content. The story is only the ticket in.

Imagine a living painting; a live portrait. The background scattered with colorful pigments while the actual place for the face is cut out of the canvas. The model places her face in its place while holding up the frame. The cheek bones, the sharp nose and deep set eyes are striking. Utterly ridiculous? Certainly, but is there a difference between this and the performance offered by the actor in a cinematic vehicle? Their performance takes the place of strips of celluloid interjecting itself as part of the art text. Where the first is evidently ludicrous and impossible to sustain (and no painter would ever consider albeit avant-gardists foray into experimental art) in cinema theater and photography have legitimatized this idea and made it into a conventional practice. In cinema, the filmmaker must modify the image of the actor, her voice, her movements, the topography of her face and body blended with the background into a dynamism where the images and sound create an audio-visual choreography that purposefully communicates. Stars and stage-ACTORS are living cutouts.

We have only the surface of a thing to consider its depth. This is the crux of art history.

Abstract paintings can be like faith in religion while the conventional posters most like a bureaucracy. A razor's edge separates them. Both are intolerable and both seductive. But the paint brush cannot pause.

A film is not a visual book. It is closer to poetry and to painting because of its free form and reliance on the juxtaposition of imagery to convey purpose and meaning.

Recently someone said that the book is always better than the movie. This is because the people making the movie want to remain "true" to the book. However, the literary aspects that made the book a 'good read' do not translate literally into a similarly dynamic visual experience. The filmmaker has to take the story, assimilate it to their experiences and find the visual codes that render it cinematically. Shakespeare's *Romeo and Juliet* and Tchaikovsky's are based on the same story but each has created it into a personal and unique form. One can never be the other. (Shakespeare's play has been sourced to a poem and novella written in the 16th century.)

People hate choice in structure but love choice in content.

Technique is a handicap for the student and the master.

There is no such thing as unconditional love ... even though I may not want to believe it. Otherwise art would not exist.

Militarization of religion and economy: The early Catholic Church, formless as it was, adopted the Roman legions attributes establishing a hierarchy of grades and ranks. (We have always tended towards militarizing most of our institutions.) In this case one creates moral postulates for its existence while the other provides structural mechanisms for action. The middle ages were the process of the amalgamation of these two concepts into the evolution of nation states. The Renaissance then added capitalism to the equation providing them with productive purpose. This tripartite has become the cornerstone of our current global cultural achievements.

A brief note on militarization: Defined hereunder it is not necessarily a concept pertaining to the military (where it is certainly most useful.) Rather, it is the establishment of a culture that sees hierarchal rule as the basis for the efficient dispatching of its purposes. Through vertically integrated control, through the adoption of strict discipline, through an authoritative process, the structure functions to accomplish what it has set out to accomplish (in our present day this is predominately related to economics.) But rather than seeing it as a social function (thereby creating mechanisms to rein its influence) its impact is to begin our immediate acculturation. It is no longer a tool but a habit forming process. When the intellect, reason, logic, loses perspective on this, bureaucratic tendencies manifest - ossification of culture takes hold. Parliamentary democracy is the militarization of the democratic process adopted by capital to facilitate the intricate complexities of an evolving global economy. We have to recognize that there is a significant difference between a tangible structure palpable and external and a structural characteristic that becomes internalized within us. When this takes place it becomes part of the DNA and therefore hidden and difficult to criticize or root out. Militarization is the Holy Ghost in the trinity with religion as the father and capitalism the son.

Ford's assembly line is a case study for the "militarization" of commodity.

Much of the color of history depends on the disposition of the story teller or maybe more on his ability to read the expressions on your face as he narrates. Can this be construed as democratic?

We communicate in absolutes. Much of our dialogues are mired in descriptive polarities. We lose a necessary sense of proportion.

Abstract art; a structure without content. A beginning or an end?

The capitalist bourgeois calculates: "while, I have in my hands lands, factories, workshops, banks; while I possess newspapers, universities, schools; while – and this most important of all – I retain control of the army: the apparatus of democracy, however, you reconstruct it, will remain obedient to my will. I subordinate to my interests spiritually the stupid, conservative, characterless lower middle class, just as it is subjected to me materially. I oppress, and will oppress, its imagination by the gigantic scale of my buildings, my transactions, my plans, and my crimes. For moments when it is dissatisfied and murmurs, I have created scores of safety-valves and lightning-conductors. At the right moment I will bring into existence opposition parties, which will disappear to-morrow, but which to-day accomplish their mission by affording the possibility of the lower middle class expressing their indignation without hurt therefrom for capitalism. I shall hold the masses of the people, under cover of compulsory general education, on the verge of complete ignorance, giving them no opportunity of rising above the level which my experts in spiritual slavery consider safe. I will corrupt, deceive, and terrorize the more privileged or the more backward of the proletariat itself. By means of these measures I shall not allow the vanguard of the working class to gain the ear of the majority of the working class, while the necessary weapons of mastery and terrorism remain in my hands." Trotsky

Religion and Capitalism are fellow travelers; they are each other's apologists.

Medievalist thought applied religious emotions (ideals regarding god and his plan) to explain observable phenomenon. In many ways, we continue to endorse such thinking to our present social/political phenomenon. By example Ptolemy's cosmology - 2nd century BCE - placed earth at the center of the universe rejecting Aristarchus' theory - 3rd century BCE - of a heliocentric universe with the planets circulating around the sun. Martianus Capella - 5th century CE - preferred to tweak the mathematical modeling of the observed data to predict and explain the apparent wandering/wobbling of the planets across the sky than consider the errors in his observations. This was in harmony with the accepted view of earth centered universe from genesis. Martianus' Quadrivium was source for scientific knowledge for almost 1000 years.

There are many historical currents that run simultaneously through any epoch often times crisscrossing and augmenting each other's effects. When a significant and noticeable shift (transition) occurs, It is important to understand the interplay of these currents (art movements, scientific thought, religious theory, economic developments, educational directions, political organizations and governance, environmental factors such as droughts, floods, fires, etc.) to appreciate their contributions, influence and changes in these transitions. The movement of economics has been demonstrated as a keen proxy to the sum of all these currents.

The Supreme Court decision in favor of Monsanto is only indicative of what it means to let structure dictate outcome. Naturally, Monsanto had every judicial and legal justification but what is the moral justification of such one sided legality? The whole process is topsy turvy. If we don't go pass the legal decision then we cannot credibly voice opposition to such one sided intrusion into something as important as creating genetic diversity of plants and foods and the primal need to work the land. There is something fundamentally wrong with Monsanto that I welcome a broad discussion. It is imperative for people to study and understand the decisions and legal rules that have chained farmers across this globe (see its impact in India) to such infuriating blinded logic.

"The least worthy thing an intellectual can do when faced with the grave events that trouble the world is to go on concerning himself with subjects that distract attention from the seriousness of those events." Antonioni

DOGMA: 1. A doctrine or a corpus of doctrines relating to matters such as morality and faith, set forth in an authoritative manner by a church. 2. An authoritative principle, belief, or statement of ideas or opinion, especially one considered to be absolutely true. 3. A principle or belief or a group of them: *"The dogmas of the quiet past are inadequate to the stormy present"* (Abraham Lincoln). All Dogmas relish quiet servitude. It is structures way of educating and infecting us with servility. It invokes a sense of permanence of things. Ultimately, it implies the belief in the inequality of people.

Don't envy other people's talents. You can't will it into you but certainly you will toil for it when it chooses you.

Even in your oldest age you will remember your mothers cooking.

Does an artist know what her canvas has in store for her today? It is a wonder the state of agitation and utter loneliness gnawing at her as she prepares for her task.

The finest pitchers men display

Are moulded out of common clay

So also is the finest verse

Moulded out of common words. - from the book, *My Daghestan*

An ideology is simply a theoretical framework to give a perspective on broad social issues. The propaganda associated with any ideology is essentially a marketing strategy to "inform." It doesn't have to provoke a negative connotation. Honesty or sincerity in this case matters. Ideation or idealizing the ideology is however problematic. There are pros and cons to any ideology that practical issues make evidently clear. It is for this reason that continuous conversation, practical experiences, and respectful but truthful dialogue without self-interest be insisted upon to prevent ideology from turning into dogma.

When two people meet on equal terms they will assimilate quite naturally. In a sense it implies a deep respect for one another which is certainly lacking in our milieu. This is one measure of the social UNIDIRECTIONAL process affecting us globally. Capitalism sees no equals.

All stories are a form of propaganda. This is true of all religious texts and heroic legends. It is this blend of mythic-reality that gives a particular group its sense of pride and cohesion, a special origin. As communication texts, then, such stories function to preserve the social ego self.

Vertical integration is what has made our species very strong and fatally weak - biologically and socially speaking.

Your point of view can never be masked. Everything is evidentiary.

One can never finish. The natural elements take care of that.

Real poetry is the ability to create a form that provides commentary to your content. This makes the piece unique to its author.

The difference between light and dark is night and day.

Peace is not a solution. It is a result. War is not a solution. It is a result.

The process that leads to action is arduous. But the initial experience that motivates must include critical thinking.

A story doesn't begin or end. You enter in the middle catching a particular thread that reverberates with you. Then you leave it for another, and another, etc. The process creates a human melody, a meta-composition.

Violence is not romantic. Choreograph it, digitalize it, justify it, commoditize it, hyper-stylize it ... violence is not romantic.

Inanimate objects are not inanimate.

Culture is the consciousness of structure.

"Why does history repeat itself?" As humans, we fail to recognize the imposition of social structures (such as culture, systems of legal bureaucracies, corporations) on the development of our character, purpose and action. This belief in complete independent thought and action is a fallacy of historical proportion. We are, as a civilization, each directed, groomed, prodded down certain channels, according to our abilities, talents and positions. The thing becomes our purpose. That thing has its own will. That thing also creates, for real human existence, violent compromises. We are cycled through the process. History repeats itself because we retain our memory and externalize our experiences into texts for future generations to study. History repeats itself because we see the contradictions. What we don't see is a dual process; our independent life form and our socially unified existence that receives its cues from the structure.

Biology 101: corporations are run by people. But corporations, like other power structures have developed a meta-conscious. Consider them as living. People, like cells, are used to maintain their function. Like cells people are differentiated into specific facilitators. Money acts as ATP to fuel the cells/people. Like a living entity corporations try to survive in an evolutionary struggle of a meta-conscious species.

Corporations and psychopaths are "incapable of feeling guilt, remorse or empathy for their actions. They are generally cunning, manipulative and know the difference between right and wrong but dismiss it as applying to them. They are incapable of normal emotions such as love, generally react without considering the consequences of their actions and show extreme egocentric and narcissistic behavior." However, corporations are a group of people, driven by profit motives, acting collectively as a psychopathic entity. The militarization process causes a mental lobotomy.

A good teacher has great patience. Patience creates space and time, a sanctuary, for ideas to gel and formulate into mental tools for their students.

If you understand historical context then you will understand that names don't matter as much as we have made them to be. People facilitate a process by the roles they assume or given them by circumstances. The conditions are created for a name to emerge. And as an aside to cinema, it is also applicable to our discussions on actors. Much of our discussions on art have deep parallels to life.

We have successfully cultivated the war on terrorism as a vital human commodity to our pursuit of economic endeavors; all this in less than one generation.

An individual is a composite of multiple "super-individual" trends and characteristics from his society. His psychology also impresses on the topography of his culture.

There has been in the debate on art history some discussion on the validity of art forms and the issue of aesthetics. To the extent that ancient arts are no longer valid contextually to the present (in the time of digital satellite communications and drone attacks vs. the gods' interference in the lives of mortals) they have continued to maintain aesthetic influence on us. [See Marx] Aestheticism (as a formal factor) has a biological relevance and its sense of permanence speaks to the human conditions that remain essentially constant within generations though our material conditions have expanded dramatically forcing new philosophical constructs to give expression to newer understandings of a universal phenomenon. Aestheticism is an internalizing mechanism.

It is not a confession without a change in direction. Otherwise it is an admission ... under duress.

Deep sorrow is something people cling to. It is neither a bad thing nor a good thing. It becomes their private core.

Absolutes are constrained within the relatives. What is valid is at the same time invalid.

The embarrassing wealth possessed by so few really doesn't amount to much from a structural view. It is access to and maintenance of devastatingly cheap labor and raped vital resources that make it all possible and necessary for the present economic structures. It is from this context that we should view the perpetual state of war that the globe is waging.

End the war on terror by ending the global war on poverty.

A Foxconn employee in China earns $400 a month working 10+ hour days six days a week making iPads for Apple. Unfortunately, these are not important details for the media. They don't connect these to transpiring events.

Trivia: the word Thursday comes from ancient Anglo-Saxon time referring to Thor's day, the son of Odin. Myths live on.

If names mattered then looking at the characters of Bush, Obama and Cheney may be constructive. They are not significantly different but of the three, Cheney understood the historical opportunity 9/11 offered his hegemonic political ideology. The rapid structural transformations he helped institute indicate that he understands structure determines content and people in the right position facilitate the turn at such moments. The other two, unable to comprehend this, have morphed into what the structure requires. Obama has been more useful as a rhetorician, apologist, or a pathetic figure. The choice words Harry Belafonte had for him and his response to him on his first inauguration suggest the vanity of a pseudo-intellectual attempting to leave his mark for posterity. His failure has been in believing in compromise – his own compromise. Bush is not oblivious as many report and he himself purports but he certainly learned it after leaving office. Most presidents do when they step away.

There is no reason not to acquire a deep political conscience. It is essential.

The total influence the Catholic Church had on Western thought in the Middle Ages confounded any ability to view the physical world in its most objective way. The world was flat; the earth was the center of the universe; the belief in a geometric logic that governed the motions of the planets was certainly errors of placing faith above the observed realities. So strong was this influence that THOUGHT, in its most general sense, stagnated. Yet, the GRAVITY of factual observations forced Kepler to doubt religious dogma. This historical detail, so often mentioned in schools, this subjugation to faith (in regards to the most tangible aspects), however, remains a persistently troubling dilemma today. Our current economic woes, political turmoil, perpetual violence in the forms of wars and conflicts, massive and epidemic poverty, environmental crisis stems from a social incapacity of people at large in developing a deep political consciousness. A desire for it has been snuffed as people's acumens for articles of FAITH continues to be sharpened; iPad, Lexus, Chanel, etc. The world is flat as far as the FAITHFUL eyes can see as they vie for modern versions of becoming deacons, priests, bishops and cardinals; to sit in a cloister, enjoy the greenery and fresh breeze, to contently contemplate the riddles of eternity.

Entertainment is political even though enormous effort is spent to disguise it.

Much of what protects the citizenry lies in the prerogatives of the fourth estate. Ideally, it is the absolute critic of the state structure including its economic engines. It intends to inform. Gathering information and offering analysis are its purpose in ensuring the contracts agreed upon by the elected and the people are kept in good faith because the power granted to so few has tremendous influence. It is for this reason the press must be free of all the same influences except the journalistic principles that bind the journalists by moral codes and ethics to its public. Understanding the mechanisms in place that subvert these vital communicative networks is a key factor in understanding our discussions on form and content and our concern about the state of the state.

Reality in science is an attempt to decipher the phenomenon of the objective facts. On the other hand, reality in art is one approach to the truth in the subjective nature of communication which defines human relationships. Power is simultaneously objective and subjective, factual and rhetorical. The reality of power relations functions within the interplay of these. Power is and has always been the issue.

A fact is not emotional. The truth is.

A commotion took place in the street one night. The man in a nearby house woke up, wrapped himself in his blanket and went out to see what the matter was. He was pulled into the mess and after a few moments everyone dispersed. He rose and noticed his blanket was missing. He returned home and his wife asked him what all the fighting was about. He said it was all about his blanket and went to bed. PERSIAN STORY

In truth, it was Sancho Panza that was a little crazy.

The body and consciousness are seemingly but distinctly disconnected yet exquisitely intimate.

There is no motion in history. Time becomes compressed behind us.

Within art we are able to define ourselves by the horizons we yearn and the place we stand. It is a unique perspective difficult to comprehend in real life.

The greatest challenge facing any artist is one of perspective.

Experience is half subjective. Are we to empty the cup or fill it?

The marriage of capitalism and nationalism ended in divorce centuries ago. Their present forays are nothing more than lust habit piled into bad TV reality shows we call the news.

A home is a living entity. It is an invested relationship. It is a solace of joy.

The Bermuda Triangle: not a place for lost planes but a tax haven for some if not most of the $32 trillion in assets (40% of global GDP) stashed away or legally laundered. Even the tax revenues from this loot could reverse the austerity programs in so many countries. It shouldn't be too difficult to place this in the context of families trying to figure out what the next item they need to purchase on their maxed out credit cards while their salaries stagnate, drop or vanish. The $32 trillion is up from the $11 trillion in 2005. This also solves the riddle of the 2008 world recession. (See: International Consortium of Investigative Journalists - ICIJ)

Simplicity can be achieved through the clear and precise representation of the complex; the whole is preserved.

The problem for many would be artists are that they seek a sense of the profound. They are too eager to play the peacock.

There is artistry in the motion of a street sweepers broom in the quiet-still asleep-morning streets.

An artist may be a liar, mean and deceitful. But to his art he will remain faithful. This is forgivable by comparison to its reciprocal which is far more common.

You can't search for poetry. It finds you.

Any image, once isolated and emphasized, becomes false. It begins to serve a different purpose. This is quite natural.

The child I was doesn't exist but my parents remain always the same.

Habits, good or bad, give the mundane aspects of life an intimate permanence; these rituals offer quiet comfort.

The artist and art historian are for obvious reasons oppositional in their work. The artist, despite the historical movements is on an utterly personal quest. Meanwhile, the art historian attempts to give inter- and intra- objective discourse to these collective subjective texts.

FINAL REFLECTIONS

(As a homage to my most cherished writer) Rasul, reach the mountain pass before night fall. The path can be treacherous in the dark. Your Aul is waiting for you. The tea is prepared in your Saklia; the Pandur hangs on the wall; we are waiting for your poems.

In reference to Michelangelo, the renaissance artist, and his Sistine Chapel I think that on a personal level it was from God that Michelangelo the man was being pulled away from and not so much him reaching to God or God breathing life into his depiction of the creation of Adam. However, the ability to capture all three movements is exhilarating to view. Nonetheless, it was this crisis that seemed to effect physically and mentally the latter part of his life. This subconscious, relative, but parallel separation was a new thing at a social level that has marked the renaissance.

Two school districts in Michigan, one in Saginaw and the other in Detroit, are being dissolved due to operating in a deficit. A no confidence in local leadership and inability to raise funds are leading to these decisions caused by the states massive spending cuts and restructuring efforts. Not a chirp from the mainstream media. I hope Prince George is well.

Bail out GM and Chrysler in Detroit. Sell out the people of Detroit.

The shoots of racial disparities sprout from the roots of economic competition.

Racial issues are not a thing on to themselves. These are symptoms of deeper systemic problems.

The French Revolution spawned two counter revolutions.

You have to obliterate the real to create the illusion of the new real. The shift is from the object (medium) to the experience (cerebral). The form becomes a vehicle to carry thoughts, feelings, emotions, etc.

Sensationalism and crisis seem to keep us preoccupied with the news. Events in the distant past have little hold on us. Yet, by way of an example, how did we leave the boundaries of the Greek city states to one of nation states? These events have tremendous implication on current events. The distant events perhaps carry more weight in giving coherence to events passing us by at digital speed.

The artist creates the illusory whole with a little bit by bit of the real.

We analyze objects but seldom the relationship of objects to each other. And here lies the secret to montage.

The impact of physical structures (implying both form and content) on character and personality are elusive and only generalizable. As a main case in point, to the extent that our planet is habitable, predicting the life forms that can or will arise is predicated by self-contained probabilities and possibilities. What is sinister is the inability for the new forms (humans) to communicate with these structures beyond evidentiary analysis through "scientific" methods. A theory of scale and time is necessary for a meta-structural narrative implying an emotional and intellectually based relationship to said facts.

Poetry's lethality is found in the sudden thrust of its tempered but agile blade.

LIE was on a walk when he met TRUTH sitting on the side of the road sulking. Why the sad face? I feel alone. Then come with me and we'll have a stroll. No, I'd rather keep my own company. Suit yourself and he continued on his way.

We don't realize the nature of our current structures is to make us complacent. Perhaps a better word is Automatism. They fundamentally remove the effort of the conscious. These usually work at the material level. Consider the dishwasher, the car, the iPhone, the security guard in the neighborhood, etc. The efficiency, the displacement of effort that these allow us, works equally at a cultural level as much as at the individual level. But these can create social tensions, predicaments and much agitation as we are forced to begin functioning at a conscious level. The Trayvon-Zimmerman case was a symptom of this.

Social Automatism is not the same as sublimation (psychological).

Every great evil was preceded by a lesser evil we became complacent with.

The study of history can't be more than a religious/mythical undertaking unless, as a historical process on to itself, it becomes a mechanism through which we reflect on our present endeavors. From this perspective history is always changing because the residue of our present mixes with our perceptions of the past. We are in a constant flux.

We only have historic permanence to anchor the present.

We make mistakes because we don't believe in mistakes.

Evolution takes a fact and creates a completely different function for it than what had been intended or designed for. The social (biologic) context for it has changed and a different purpose becomes apparent. This is true on a genetic level as much as artistic or macro-social level. On a social level this is called a revolution.

A film maker thinks more like a painter than a photographer. One is an asset the other a limitation.

e.g. Marvel Comics and Hollywood popular genres: Once a FORMula works it is only a matter of giving the same experience to this popular art through recurring themes. The FORM becomes inconspicuous. The experience becomes only emotional as the formal features are in large measure calculated and preconditioned losing their extraneous conscious imposition on the content. In a manner of speaking, this is the closest we get to separating form and content by negating the formal experience. (The negation occurs through repetition.)

Urbanization, as a formal social industrializing process, has distanced us through the decades from fundamental bio-social relationships. Our current activities, utterly ridiculous and lacking purpose though at the same time seeming so necessary, are difficult to abandon. We bought the house and now own the debt. This debt, both real and imaginary, conditions our reality away from the critical tasks at hand.

Republicans/libertarians work under the premise of folk-politics, a belief that social functions are "an outcome of deep-seated drives allowing nothing to external influences." In this sense, democrats are more realistic as corporate apologists and fellow travelers.

What is relativism and absolutism? Relativism is the infinite planes intersecting each other to create a sphere. Absolutism is one tangential plane to a point on the surface of the sphere. The absolute came first but functions as a non-reality.

A man's position is often times put into contradiction to his person. He often times betrays his person.

No federal support for Detroit's bankruptcy. New Orleans faced an environmental hurricane while Detroit an economic one. The response to the crisis (not of their doing) is the same. People who have no material value are deemed valueless.

"Live the dream" is a perfidious trap.

Popular art caters to a passive public doling out uncreative artistic goods disguised behind their high production value.

Imposition of social isolation through the channels of mass media is a very effective herding strategy driving the apoliticism we are encountering.

In a drawing the line is the illusion. It is really the place of action created between negative and positive space. With color this takes on exponential proportions. In science they call this the gravitational field.

"...loneliness is a social category and that as an individual experience it can exist only in a society." Arnold Hauser

Formal aspects in art expand or contract within the space and time the present allows often times being spawned or becoming extinct almost chaotically. Art history then attempts to impose a thread of order to them in the compressed past looking for a unifying theory that can explain these random developments. A clear social link between the artist, movements in their art, economic and political developments is nearly impossible or fatal to attempt. Yet, the answer lies only there. And even still these historical reflections are more an attempt at a social self-discovery in what we concretely have termed the present.

Art texts don't create echoes. They are echoes.

How much of "my" narrative is based on a much larger cultural narrative I blindly accept, a social narrative thrust upon me, not like clothing but like grafted skin.

To have peace you have to abandon your fears. To abandon your fears you have to develop trust. To develop trust you have to want to share.

Why does history repeat itself? I forgot.

Art is not nature because art is always fictitious. To make art seem natural is to hide the fiction.

The line between representation and expression is a difficult one. Formal measures as in the flat paintings of the Christian Middle Ages clearly demarcate the difference between 'sign' and 'copy'. The naturalist rendition as seen in the renaissance obscures this but the expressions of religious tension is none the less evident. Representation and expression merge.

It isn't that natural phenomena and experience are not considered credible but that they are deemed insignificant in comparison to the 'order' of things as in religious doctrine or even imperial hubris. This perspective has spanned human civilization.

To harp again on "collaborative art" it is now considered a truism and for many an irrefutable fact. Yet this remains the most erroneous and (in my opinion) sinister construct. I naturally speak on a FORMal level. Those that accept collaborative art, those artists or critics and friends of the art, simply do not understand the FORMal mechanism of art unable to distinguish the medium from its linguistics. If they wished to defend their position, they could better argue by referencing the evolutionary development of formal technique within art movements as established by various schools, guilds and institutions that have fostered particular techniques that said artists adopt and adapt. Imitation or borrowing is rampant. It is human. This historic collaboration is far more compelling than a façade of artisans engaged predominately on what I call the aesthetic aspects of art for commercial purposes. The Sistine Chapel belongs to Michelangelo. His Pieta is his as much as David has been conceived through his depiction regardless of the papal commissions and prerogatives. Artists work within the structures that open to them.

This particular but secondary issue continues to be a socio-economically and politically charged aspect of our historic artistic development. Moving ahead to cinema, there has been no other quite like the three giants; Vertov, Bresson and Antonioni. What separates them from the Hollywood frame of mind is that they not only understood the intricacy of their form they also understood the balance between artificiality of all artistic texts contained within the utmost desire for sincere self-expression within climates that rejected such authorship. They were intimately involved in every aspect of the construction of their audio-visual pieces; the choice of location, the story, the models, ambient noises, shots and angles, script, the cuts … every cut that was insisted upon. The behind the scene battles are forgotten legends. There was no collaborative effort that pieced it together.

No idyllic universal themes or narrative formulas and sleek aesthetic experiences that is quite commonplace and achievable in collaborative efforts. Vertov, Bresson and Antonioni surprise you. They create something unexperienced. They show themselves and not what you may want to see. From this consideration we also must recognize that democracy as a collaborative endeavor can only begin with a genuine experience in communication. What we develop from this is diversity in "species" instead of the perfect genetically modified flower.

The growth of towns and cities circa 11th century led to the transition from a trade in goods to a money economy. With this process came banking, taxation, and centralization of production. Land and its resources became vital for this transition including the ideas of nation building and the development of a national conscience among the denizens. It is also interesting to note that intellectual development, though confined to monastic studies, made a course towards reason over irrationality as a byproduct of this transformation. However, for the masses, magical thinking persists.

The influences of dominant nations on developing nations through international channels begin to color the cultural developments and attitudes of those people arguably interfering with it. However there is barely any contact between the people of these nations.

We are fed on factory fabricated fictionalized narratives like the output of fast food industry eager to jack up the trans-fat and sugar high in our efficient and ready-made meals. We suffer from a diabetic stupor of conscience and artery clogging social ineptitude.

We have developed very filmic emotional expressions but remain undeveloped in filmic thinking.

It strikes me as ... comical ... that the cuts in SNAP are reportedly driven by "limited resources" and need for efficiency while the number of billionaires since 2009 has doubled in the world whose assets total in the trillions.

The scope of last week's politics on both the national and international stages stands in stark relief to the environmental disaster that has shed such untold misery in the Philippines. It is a page out of history that needs careful study.

How many degrees of separation (self-deception) does it take ... to relinquish responsibility.

The right answer is always ignored.

We watch the world through the prisms of a television set; the measure of democracy the number of channels; the weight of the images draw our eyes and our necks follow.

What was compelling in the documentary film "the square" was the murals being painted as the Egyptian revolution was progressing giving present history a present and evolving artistic rendition.

Political coalitions are by analysis dubious endeavors if the socioeconomic issues remain persistent or entrenched. They are nothing more than a cast of flunkies uniting as a power bloc only to later split as factions in an internal strife to wrest from each other what they previously agreed to uphold. It is ludicrous how they rhetorically, like minstrels and bards poetically serenading romantic love, aspire to work together for a common cause while celebrating in the brothels. What made the Reagan era seem nostalgic was the brash and criminal neocon agenda of economic pillaging that enriched so many of the so few. Now a cancer is eating out the innards of this monstrosity. Failed coalitions attempting to unite what?

We don't kill by killing. We kill by over populating one species with another. It has been this way with civilizations. It is true with corporations and how they impoverish with their wealth. It is true with culture and mass produced commodities. Like cancer cells we overwhelm the truth with an abundance of lies until the truth no longer exists. This has not been understood well by many though they have felt it often. It has a term - annihilation.

Spontaneity is ultimately dependent on convention. It cannot be any other way. It is how opposition in art is defined.

We eat cuisines from all over the world but try to keep *those* people out.

" ... *the next attempt of the French Revolution will be no longer ... to transfer the bureaucratic-military machine from one hand to another, but to smash it and it is essential for every real people's revolution on the continent*." Karl Marx, from *Letters to Dr. Kugelmann on the Paris Commune, April 12, 1871.*

Every revolutionary assimilates the lessons of revolutionary experience for the future. Lenin's analysis of Marx's commentary was a vital next step. He learned from Marx that past structures when commandeered from their predecessors create only a similar content and that the revolution needs to smash these old structures if it hopes to develop new and more sincere content. Lenin also understood that by *people* Marx implied all classes engaged in a revolutionary cause including the peasantry, workers, small businessmen, artist, teachers, lawyers, etc. despite their natural but fraudulent class antagonism. If a bourgeoisie milieu undergoes such a revolution the classes engaged will also transform as the new milieu dictates – the structure of a new classless society will transform these same people as the experience will acculturate them towards the new conditions. These new conditions, however, carry with them a heavy baggage of historical inertia. It was Trotsky that grasped this, years before the October revolution, the nature [as I have come to understand it] of permanent revolution.

The civil war, the lack of productive resources, the lack of time was cause for the turn to bureaucracy which subverted the intentions of the revolution. The Soviet Union became a working class state under siege until its implosion and final demise. It is only through the theory of permanent revolution can we explicate socialism from Stalin's inept, sinister and disastrous tyranny and ruinous public relations for the cause of working class struggle. Until now, the present current economic endeavors have spent enormous efforts to dispense privilege while apoliticizing a broad section of the public. Productive capacities have been internationalized, isolated, separated and vertically integrated disabling humanity from interacting within the capacity of the *proletariat*. Also, a tremendous onslaught of propaganda has been generated through covert coercive and overt militaristic pressures to bear on maintaining allegiances with the corporate philosophy.

In this context, the corporate philosophy has assimilated Marxist social theories better than the working class to create their own weapons against socialism.

By example, the spontaneous Arab Spring revolution in Egypt, its failure, demonstrated with historic precision Marx's observations and cautionary statements. Still, the socialist experiments and aberrations that have evolved around various parts of the globe in the last century since the Soviet Union require careful observation within the framework of a permanent global revolution. We have to understand that these infant societies need time to develop experience; time to practice; time to circumnavigate the colossal impediments placed in their way. It is to this cause that we need to maintain unflinching vigilance. It is the only way to guard ourselves against the economic barbarism that is hurling at each one of us.

Imperialism: The historical development of an undeveloped country in a capitalist milieu does not follow a linear relationship.

There is no mathematical modeling of these. You certainly can't place a pattern of one over the other expecting similar results. These international influences and connections advances one and the other within specific conduits at one instance while, generally speaking, negatively effecting other aspects creating still new conditions otherwise unexperienced; new lessons are learned and applied. Imperialism, the advanced stage of capitalism, as Lenin had called it, requires a deepening of our theoretical understanding of it recognizing the real and practical conditions that influence the haphazard trajectory of this monstrosity.

It requires putting in context the manner in which the capitalist productive forces imprints these conditions on our collective psyches; the rhetoric of freedom and democratization of the globe through the commodification of terrorism in its socio-economic sense [at present], the stupefaction of a minority of its influential citizenry while subordinating the under privileged and working classes to accept slave labor as a means for their salvation, the never-ending degeneration of artistic and educational development so vital to social organisms' progress, the utilization of legalistic shenanigans to justify the methods used to confiscate the resources necessary for life by way of parliamentary politics, financial bankruptcy and out right militaristic force.

In short, the violence it projects in its assent towards global domination can only be confounded by and confronted through what Marx called the dictatorship of the proletariat which implies the violent overthrow of imperialism as a method of capitalist development that holds humanity hostage as its necessary life force. It is imperative that this dictatorship put into context the present lack of intelligent and humane balance of our productive resources which will require their resolute and precise clarity of vision and indomitable will to understand what has to be done.

The atomization of individuals functioning in society has found representation in the most formless of abstract art. It is against this trend that artists must see, find and confront these tendencies to capitulate. Post modernists and structuralists need to move towards a new formulation that splits [*smashes*] this atom.

MIST

A morning mist

Insinuates itself

Between sleeping trees

And manicured lawns

Cold droplets of dew

Cling to still dark windows

Till heavy with 'wait'

Then gravity

Sets them in motion

EPILOGUE

The intention of offering these vignettes in a book format was in large part a need to bring analysis back to what amounts to the persistent militarization/automation of our social consciousness. I have attempted to create ideas regarding these issues than to give explanatory notes. My hope was for the reader to attempt to reconstruct these ideas into a logical coherency and personal position statements and whether they agreed, disagreed or offered alternative postulate was not in the purview of my purpose though the intent is in defense of socialism and Marx's methodology.

Fundamentally, communication is the only faculty that brings social context to humanities existence. The sum of our social consciousness is contained within the activities that constitute communication. Beyond its basic definition, communication entails a broad scope of activities that more often are contained in action than rhetoric. To understand the fundamentals of social consciousness it requires a clear demarcation of the ideas behind form and content and recognizing, art being one discipline where form and content are consistently discussed and analyzed, that all political, religious and social structures ultimately are designed for communicative purposes.

In this sense economics is the discipline for the communicative purpose of the material conditions of human life and has come to dominate and influence all aspects of our intellectual and physical existence. It is from this aspect that it becomes important for the reader to understand that events have to be integrated into a whole instead of parsed down into its miniscule sub-divisions to appreciate the context of all human activities. From this perspective, our infra-structures, our material conditions, our system of laws and their enforcement, condition our culture and create our beliefs and attitudes. Culture is a communicative process. It is the conscious and conscience of structure.

However, what we currently lack is the awareness that what constitutes our individuality is conditioned in large part by structure. Naturally, every individual is unique and specific in their own way and it is not intended to negate this very important aspect. Our uniqueness is something very important to celebrate. But it must be recognized that an individual born in a place, a certain time, a certain gender, a certain class, a certain race, will develop in certain predictable ways. And as structures have become more flexible and complex the method for indoctrinating has become much more subtle and indirect as compared to a more rigid and totalitarian manner.

These can be seen in our educational systems, work, church, entertainment, and political structures. Though we constantly hark on our individual rights and liberties, we are constantly reminded about what constitutes the ideal person; physically fit, handsome, cheery, hardworking, pride in nation and country, etc. To the extent we fit or don't is no longer so much dictated by structure but by the citizenry that imposes a moral dictum on itself. Structure sublimates and people enforce. This becomes much more insidious to challenge because of its pseudo-democratic appearance.

Let us review some recent events in the news to give clearer picture of these. Recently The Supreme Court of the United States (SCOTUS) has struck down section three of the Defense of Marriage Act that has been seen as a tremendous progress to giving same sex couples equality under the law. In the same breath SCOTUS also chiseled at the foundation of affirmative action by abstaining from giving a clear position on this issue essentially stating that racial issues have now been cleansed from the U.S. Meanwhile the right to obtain DNA from people yet to be convicted of a crime or allowing the provisions from the Patriot Act to lead to issues of NSA and secret wiretapping and killing of citizens with drone strikes without a trial speaks to structures defense of privilege as a proxy to upholding equality under the law.

Yet, there is little uproar or action from the citizenry that challenges these structural imposition on our communities or societies. Putting context to all these we must admit that capitalist structures, the present imperialist economic endeavors of this structure, is ridding its body of any contradictions based on the obvious aspects of race or gender as it subsumes them into its purpose. The SCOTUS decisions or lack of position, as mentioned above, protects structure from its own potential over reach by defending privileges. Defense of privileges arbitrarily negates issues that deal with equality or humanity.

We have all come to assume these are one and the same but present evidence from the economic turmoil faced by people in every nation remains the largest contradiction to this ridiculous dictum. The institution of defense of privilege removes from people what needs to be most emboldened within them – their sense of justice. This is the surest way to create a people that are not united nor can communicate as a social entity as one person. And without a participating citizenship that controls the reign of structure we remain non-existent. We therefore come to function for structure as our purpose.

YOU WILL KNOW CAIN

If you begin to measure your life against another man's

Then you will know Cain

These blue mountains of ice and snow

Fragile, delicate and so seductive

And yet your whispers will send the avalanche thundering upon us

Burying us into a deeper silence

One colder than we could ever know

And if we should survive … stunned and broken

Will we be pawns left half buried with hollowed cores?

Knowing he was our brother

He was ours

A panicked voice calls out from the dark

"In your enemies eyes you can see your own reflection."

ABOUT THE AUTHOR

Who I am is unimportant.